IDEAS BEHIND THE MODERN CHESS OPENINGS

ATTACKING WITH WHITE

GARY LANE

B.T. Batsford Ltd, *London*

First published in 2002
© Gary Lane 2002

ISBN 0 7134 8712 7

British Library Cataloguing-in-Publication Data.
A catalogue record for this book is
available from the British Library.

Printed in Great Britain by
Creative Print and Design (Wales), Ebbw Vale
for the publishers,
B.T. Batsford Ltd,
64 Brewery Road,
London N7 9NT

A member of **Chrysalis** Books plc

Dedicated to Dr. Sanmogam Goundar

*With thanks to Ashley Silson and François Mertens
for their help in providing material for this book.*

A BATSFORD CHESS BOOK

CONTENTS

INDEX OF GAMES

INTRODUCTION

The idea of this book is to cover everything that White needs to know in order to play 1 d4 with confidence. There is an emphasis on learning key plans and ideas rather than remembering vast numbers of moves. As a basis for White's opening strategy I am suggesting the London System, which is suitable for those with a limited amount of time for study and who wish to play something reliable yet with attacking prospects.

HISTORY OF THE LONDON SYSTEM

The London tournament of 1922 was a top class event with its games hitting the world chess headlines of the day. Among the openings regularly employed—against a variety of set-ups by Black—was White's formation of **1 d4**, **2 ♘f3** and **3 ♗f4**, subsequently christened the 'London system'. Though long regarded as a solid option with chances of aggressive play on the kingside, it has remained in the shadows for years due to the popularity of other openings such as the Queen's Gambit and main line King's Indian Defence. However a sizeable number of contemporary players, looking for something 'new' with plenty of scope for improvement on standard lines, have recently boosted the popularity of this underestimated opening both at club and international level.

IDEAS BEHIND THE OPENING

This is the piece development that White intends to employ against just about everything! The big attraction of the opening is that an understanding of the key ideas makes it easy to play and to obtain promising middle-game positions. A standard continuation for White is e2-e3, ♗d3, 0-0 and ♘bd2, after which, having mobilised the minor pieces, there are a number of ways to proceed such as ♘f3-e5 followed by a transfer of the queen to the kingside for an attack.

White's opening choice is perfect for those who want to cut down on their learning time because—regardless of how Black responds—a grasp of the general ideas depicted in the main games should allow players to handle any situations that may arise. You might say that 'connoisseurs select it—experts perfect it!'

Tseitlin-Liesmann
Kleve 1999

1 d4 d5 2 ♘f3 ♘f6 3 ♗f4 e6 4 e3 ♗e7 5 ♘bd2 c5 6 c3 0-0 7 ♗d3

This is the basic position of the London System with White having swiftly developed his pieces and prepared kingside castling. The pawn on d4 is ably supported by the c and e pawns. A set-up that can be adopted against practically every black defence, thus making White's opening preparation a good deal easier than usual!

7...♘c6 8 0-0 b6 9 ♘e5 ♗b7 10 ♕f3 ♖c8 11 ♖ad1 ♘b8 12 ♖fe1 ♘bd7 13 ♕h3 ♖e8 14 ♘df3 h6

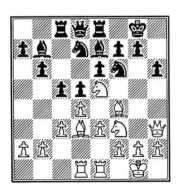

White has managed to create a strong attack by transferring his queen to the kingside in preparation for a breakthrough.

15 ♗xh6! gxh6 16 ♕g3+ ♔f8 17 ♘xf7 ♔xf7 18 ♕g6+ ♔f8 19 ♕xh6+ ♔g8 20 ♕g6+ ♔h8 21 ♘g5 1-0

A deeper analysis of the game can be found in the chapter 'The London System'.

A GUIDE TO THE BACKBONE OF THE OPENINGS

The ideas behind the London System can be used against a variety of Black defences.

BEATING THE CHIGORIN

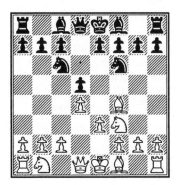

White adopts the standard set-up of developing the queen's bishop and king's knight. This works perfectly against the Chigorin since now Black is frustrated in his attempt to play the liberating ...e7-e5.

DEFEATING THE DUTCH

I have paid special attention to the Dutch Defence because it is a favourite of club players everywhere. I recommend an early ♗f4 against the Classical set-up but the peculiarities of the Leningrad Dutch demand a different approach so I propose the following straightforward line for White.

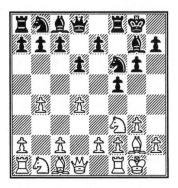

The advance of the b-pawn might look odd but it is a fashionable line played even by such top grandmasters as Anand and Van Wely.

DEALING WITH 1...♞F6

In the chapters on the Anti-Benoni and Pseudo-Benko I could not apply the London System. I have therefore made an effort to side-step main lines by keeping faith, whenever possible, with my basic principle of avoiding c2-c4 in the opening stage—the advantage being that White remains on familiar ground whereas Black is unable to transpose into main lines.

The London System can certainly also work well against 1...♞f6. For example, a popular defence is the Nimzo-Indian but when White omits c2-c4 and plays 2 ♞f3, denying Black this option, he usually resorts to the Queen's Indian instead. This formation is adequately covered. For example, in the game Christiansen-D.Gurevich it should be clear to any experienced 'London' player why White was able to develop his pieces so rapidly in readiness for the forthcoming middlegame battle.

1 d4 ♞f6 2 ♞f3 e6 3 ♝f4 b6 4 e3 c5 5 ♝d3 ♝b7 6 c3

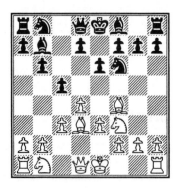

A standard set-up for White and proof that even if you do not have detailed knowledge of 'variations' it is possible to play the opening with confidence.

The Grünfeld chapter demonstrates that when Black plays the customary ...d5 he is denied his usual traps or tricks because there is no longer any challenge to a white pawn on c4. In fact the position is quite different and allows White to calmly get on with the job of developing.

Anyone who plays the King's Indian Defence likes the opening because it is replete with tactics and counterattacking chances. However the solid London system frustrates most of Black's ambitions whilst retaining most of his own!

Payen-Gross
New York 1999

1 d4 ♘f6 2 ♘f3 g6 3 ♗f4 ♗g7 4 e3 d6 5 h3 0-0 6 ♗e2 ♘bd7 7 0-0 ♕e8

This queen move looks odd but Black wants to advance his e-pawn.

8 ♗h2 e5 9 c4 ♘e4 10 ♘bd2 ♘xd2 11 ♕xd2 e4 12 ♘e1 ♕e7 13 ♘c2 f5 14 ♕a5

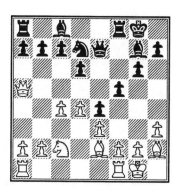

This is an improvement on an old game mentioned in the 'books' and certainly flummoxed Black who now proceeded to give away his pawns...

14...♘f6 15 c5 g5 16 cxd6 cxd6 17 ♘a3 b5 18 ♕b4 ♘e8 19 ♗xb5 f4 20 ♗xe8 ♕xe8 21 ♕xd6 ♗a6 22 ♖fc1 fxe3 23 fxe3 ♕f7 24 ♗g3 ♖ad8 25 ♖c7 ♕f1+ 26 ♖xf1 ♖xf1+ 27 ♔h2 ♖xd6 28 ♗xd6 ♖e1 29 ♘c2 ♖e2 30 ♘b4 ♗d3 31 ♘d5 ♖c2 32 ♖xa7 ♗f1 33 ♗e5 ♗xe5+ 34 dxe5 ♗xg2 35 ♘f6+ ♔f8 36 e6 1-0

THE BARRY ATTACK

The London System is perfectly good against the ever popular King's Indian Defence and the chapter on it should inspire White players. However I wanted to add another option in the form of the Barry Attack.

This is a speciality of English practitioners who have employed it with success even at international level. King's Indian specialists find it awkward because, if they decline to play the usual …d7-d6 and reply …d7-d5, they find themselves lured into a different type of position and faced with the tactically orientated Barry Attack. If Black replies with …d7-d6 in the diagrammed position then e4 enters the Pirc, which will probably not suit him unless he is in the habit of meeting 1 e4 with 1…d6. Moreover Black's misery will be compounded if White is allowed to unleash the dreaded '150 Attack'—recently jokingly upgraded to the '2800 Attack' after Kasparov's use of it to demolish Radjabov in the final of the FIDE Grand Prix in Moscow 2002. I devote a chapter to explaining the ideas of this alive and extremely dangerous weapon.

AN OVERNIGHT SENSATION

If you are wondering whether you have the time or inclination to learn the London System then be encouraged by the fact that somebody once dropped their 1 e4 openings to play it and then went on to become world champion!

When a teenage Garry Kasparov had to play a vital game at the prestigious Soviet junior championship he decided to play 1 d4 for only the second time in his life. Of course it is not possible to learn a mass of opening theory overnight so he opted for the London System which can be played against almost all the main lines. In his video biography he commented "I had very limited knowledge of the opening after 1 d4. That's why I tried to develop all of the pieces and have a solid position and hope that later I could use my tactical superiority." If it is good enough for Kasparov then it should be good enough for mere mortals with limited time to study.

Kasparov-Kengis
USSR Under 20 Championship, Riga 1977

1 d4 ♘f6 2 ♘f3 b6 3 ♗f4 ♗b7 4 e3 c5 5 ♘bd2 g6 6 c3 ♗g7 7 h3 0-0 8 ♗e2

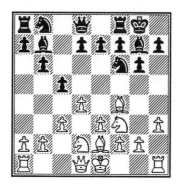

8...♘c6 9 0-0 d6 10 a4 a6 11 ♘c4 b5! 12 ♘a3

"Black is losing the battle on the queenside so he has to find some active moves."

12...b4 13 cxb4 ♘xb4 14 dxc5 ♘fd5 15 cxd6 ♗xb2

"Kengis was not looking for compensation—he was there to kill."

16 ♗h6 ♖e8

Black is happy to move the rook because he has no wish to trade this piece for its 'trapped' counterpart on a1. But...

17 d7!

The move that Kengis missed! White entices the black queen to an unfavourable square.

17...♕xd7 18 ♘c4 ♗xa1 19 ♕xa1 e5?!

19...f6 is the sternest defence although after 20 e4 White is better. However Kasparov was not surprised that his opponent rejected the defence linked to 19...f6 because, in his mind, Black felt close to victory even though that moment had gone. In the words of Kasparov ...f6 was rejected because "Instead of dreaming about attack and about initiative, Black is reduced to a very passive and unpleasant defence".

20 ♘cxe5 ♕e6 21 ♘g4

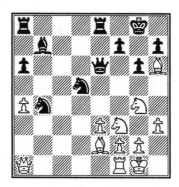

The queen's knight has been suitably transformed from a spectator on a3 to a main participant on g4—a striking example of the value of active pieces.

21...f6 22 ♗c4

The pin on the knight, carrying the primary threat of ♘xf6+, is decisive.

22...♖f8 23 e4 1-0

I would not dare suggest that playing the London System and my recommended lines leads exclusively to forced wins for White! In fact I am sure that improvements on Black's play can be found in the games. However I do want to show the power of White's attacking possibilities and convince the reader that the openings in this book are easy to learn but difficult to beat.

THE LONDON SYSTEM

The London System is one of White's most dependable openings, promising rapid development and a solid pawn formation. There are also real possibilities for a kingside attack which has attracted players such as Hodgson, Kasparov and Yusupov. In the introduction we have already given a historical perspective and an outline of the ideas behind the opening.

HOW TO WIN WITH THE LONDON SYSTEM

White's opening choice enables a swift development of pieces, often in preparation for a kingside attack. The main games offer ample evidence of this aggressive intent.

Tseitlin-Liesmann
Kleve 1999

1 d4 d5 2 ♘f3 ♘f6 3 ♗f4 e6

A quiet plan. Black just wants to proceed with his kingside development along the lines of a standard Queen's Gambit Declined.

4 e3 ♗e7

4...♗d6, to offer an exchange of bishops, is discussed in the next game.

5 ♘bd2 c5 6 c3

Generally speaking White will meet any …c7-c5 advance with c3. The reason being that White wants to maintain a pawn formation that stops Black's pieces from invading on the queenside. It is worth remembering that if Black captures on d4 then White takes back with the e-pawn, thereby allowing him to exert more control on the important e5 square after, for example, kingside castling and ♖e1.

6…0-0 7 ♗d3 ♘c6 8 0-0

8…b6

Black chooses to employ a queenside fianchetto in order to help mobilise his queenside forces. On the other hand, 8…c4?! is a typical mistake in such positions. Black has hopes of closing the centre and launching a queenside pawn storm after 9 ♗b1 b5. But then comes 10 e4! (the right reaction—by advancing the e-pawn White can either open up the game for his pieces or push the pawn forward one more square to kick away the key defensive knight) 10…♗b7 11 e5 ♘h5 (perhaps 11…♘d7!? although 12 ♕c2 g6 13 ♗h6 ♖e8 14 ♖e1 offers White the better chances) 12 ♗e3 f6? 13 g4 when, much to his embarrassment, Black finds his king's knight is trapped, Esposito-Maupin, Pau 2000. Also possible is 8…♘h5, to exchange White's dark-squared bishop, when Belamarić-Solić, Pula 2000, continued 9 dxc5 (9 ♗g3 is a safe choice) 9…♘xf4 10 exf4 h6!? (10…♗xc5 is possible when 11 ♗xh7+ ♔xh7 12 ♘g5+ ♔h6 leaves White still having to prove that his attack is worth a piece) 11 ♘b3 ♕c7 12 ♕d2 ♘b8 13 ♗c2 ♘d7 (if 13…♗xc5 then 14 ♘xc5 ♕xc5 15 ♕d3 g6 16 ♘e5, threatening ♘xg6, gives White a fine game) 14 ♖fe1 ♗xc5 15 ♘xc5 ♕xc5 16 ♘e5 ♘f6 17 g4 intending g4-g5 is a sharp idea.

9 ♘e5 ♗b7

9…♘xe5 has been tested although after 10 dxe5 the knight on f6 must relinquish its defensive duties on f6 by retreating 10…♘d7. Then comes 11 ♕g4 (the queen is brought into the attack with the primary threat of 12 ♗h6) 11…♖e8 12 ♘f3 ♘f8 (12…♗f8? walks into 13 ♗xh7+ ♔xh7 14 ♘g5+ ♔g8 15 ♕h5 winning) 13 h4 f5 14 exf6 ♗xf6 15 ♕g3 ♕e7 16 ♗d6

♛f7 17 e4 ♝b7 18 e5 ♝d8 19 ♝b5! (the pressure on the kingside has forced Black to take defensive action which leaves his pieces in a state of disharmony) 19...♞d7 20 ♞g5 ♝xg5 21 hxg5 a6 22 ♝a4 b5 23 ♝c2 ♜ac8? (oops!) 24 g6 1-0 Mawira-Ensdorp, Haarlem 2000.

10 ♛f3

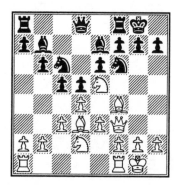

This queen move came as a surprise to Black who now appears content to shuffle his pieces around the board. On the other hand White gives notice that he is ready to attack by transferring the queen to the kingside. A dream position for London players because it is solid but latently aggressive.

10...♜c8

Black brings the queen's rook to a more active square. Others:

a) 10...♝d6?! (moving the bishop twice in the opening for no apparent reason cannot be right) 11 ♛h3 ♞e7 12 ♜ad1 ♛e8? 13 ♞g4! 1-0 Kock-Sucher, Liechtenstein 1992.

b) 10...♞d7 (Black seeks exchanges in an attempt to reduce the impact of the attack) 11 ♛h3 f5 12 ♞df3 ♞dxe5 13 ♞xe5 ♞xe5 14 ♝xe5 ♛e8 15 f4 (giving White a comfortable edge due to his space advantage) 15...cxd4 16 exd4 ♝c6 17 ♜f3 (now comes a model example of how to increase the pressure on an opponent's position) 17...♝f6 18 ♜e1 (the queen's rook comes to the centre in order to apply pressure on the backward e6 pawn) 18...♝xe5 19 ♜xe5 ♜f6 20 ♜fe3 ♛d7 21 ♛h5 ♜e8 22 ♛e2 ♔f7 23 ♜h3 ♔g8 24 g4! (a thematic idea that will come as a natural reaction to any London specialist—in a closed position it is perfectly reasonable to advance flank pawns!) 24...fxg4 25 ♝xh7+ ♔f8 26 ♛xg4 ♛f7 27 ♝d3 ♜xf4 28 ♛g2 ♜f6 29 ♜g5 1-0 Cibulka-Hrusković, Slovakian Team Ch 1997.

11 ♜ad1 ♞b8?!

Liesmann runs out of constructive moves and is inspired to manoeuvre his knight via b8 to d7 from where it might lend support to the king by proceeding to f8. The text also uncovers the bishop on b7 to keep an eye on the advance e3-e4. However 11...♞xe5 also does little to reduce the pressure after 12 dxe5 ♞d7 13 ♕h3 when White is better.

12 ♖fe1 ♞bd7 13 ♕h3

The queen targets the h7 pawn—now all White has to do is get rid of the defending knight on f6. Though this sounds easy there is still some work to do before victory is in sight. White's main trump is that he has plenty of active pieces which provide him with various attacking options.

13...♖e8

Black is hoping to ease the pressure on h7 by making room for his knight to go to f8.

14 ♞df3 h6

An understandable reaction to stop White occupying the g5 square. Thus an immediate 14...♞f8 would allow 15 ♞g5, targeting f7 and leaving Black unable to defend this pawn.

15 ♗xh6!

A star move, ripping apart Black's flimsy pawn barrier and enabling the white queen to invade and destroy.

15...gxh6 16 ♕g3+ ♚f8 17 ♞xf7!

Tseitlin makes a second sacrifice which places the black king under even closer scrutiny from the menacing white pieces.

17...♚xf7

The cool approach is 17...♕c7 although after 18 ♕g6 White maintains an excellent position.

18 ♕g6+ ♚f8 19 ♕xh6+ ♚g8 20 ♕g6+ ♚h8 21 ♞g5 1-0

Black did not want to see 21...♖f8 22 ♕h6+ ♚g8 23 ♗h7+ ♚h8 24 ♗f5+ ♚g8 25 ♗xe6+ ♖f7 26 ♗xf7 mate.

Black can also offer an exchange of the dark-squared bishops in an effort to fight for control of the e5 square.

Kocovski-Mitkov
La Coruna 1995

1 d4 ♘f6 2 ♘f3 d5 3 ♗f4 e6 4 e3 ♗d6

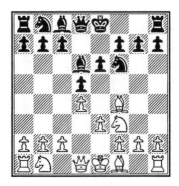

A reliable but tame response which hopes to challenge for control of the e5 square and reduce White's attacking options by exchanging dark-squared bishops.

5 ♗g3

I think this is the easiest way to deal with the offer to exchange bishops. Now at least, if the bishop on g3 is taken, White can recapture with the h-pawn which will leave the king's rook on an open file ready for potential tactical opportunities. Of course, depending on how Black responds, White still has the option of castling behind a solid wall of pawns on the kingside, if he does not want to lead his king to shelter on the other flank. I have also taken a close look at 5 ♘bd2, 5 ♗d3 and 5 ♗xd6 but if White wants an alternative line I would recommend 5 ♘e5 on the basis that at least Black is denied any immediate trade of bishops. For example:

a) 5...♘bd7 6 ♗d3 c5? (surprisingly, quite a few people have fallen for this trap) 7 ♘xf7! ♔xf7 8 ♗xd6 ♕b6 9 dxc5 ♕xb2 10 ♘d2 when the misplaced black king gives White the better chances.

b) 5...0-0 6 ♗d3 c5 7 c3 ♘c6 8 ♘d2 ♗xe5 9 dxe5 ♘d7 10 ♘f3 (10 ♕g4 ♘dxe5 11 ♗xe5 ♘xe5 12 ♗xh7+ ♔xh7 13 ♕h5+ ♔g8 14 ♕xe5 is roughly equal) 10...h6 11 ♗g3 (11 ♗c2 is a more aggressive option when the natural 11...♕c7?! runs into 12 ♕d3 giving White the superior chances because of the threat of ♕h7+) 11...♕c7 12 0-0 ♘dxe5 13 e4 (White has sacrificed a pawn but in return has the initiative) 13...♘xf3+ 14 ♕xf3 ♕d8

15 ♖ad1 d4 (15...dxe4 does nothing to ease the tension since after 16 ♕xe4 f5 17 ♕e3 ♕b6 18 ♖d2, intending ♗d6, is fine for White) 16 e5 ♕d5 17 ♕e2 b6 (17...♕xa2?! allows a strong white attack after 18 ♕e4 g6 19 cxd4 cxd4 20 ♕h4 h5 21 ♗f4! ♕xb2 22 ♗h6, intending ♕f6 with a winning advantage) 18 ♗e4 ♕d7 19 cxd4 cxd4 (19...♘xd4? 20 ♖xd4 ♕xd4 21 ♗xa8 wins a piece) 20 ♗f4 ♗b7 21 ♗xh6! ♘e7 (acceptance of the sacrifice by 21...gxh6 implies that Black accepts the repetition 22 ♕g4+ ♔h8 23 ♕h4 ♔g7 24 ♕g4+) 22 ♗g5 ♗xe4 23 ♕xe4 ♕d5 24 ♕g4 ♘g6 ½-½ Bellini-Arlandi, Corridonia 2000.

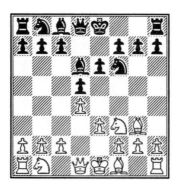

5...♘e4

Black wants to exchange the bishop but without surrendering his bishop pair. Others:

a) 5...0-0 6 ♗d3 c5 7 c3 when play might continue:

a1) 7...♘c6 8 ♘bd2 ♕e7 9 ♘e5 ♗xe5 10 dxe5 ♘d7 11 f4 f6 offers equal chances.

a2) 7...b6 8 ♘bd2 ♗a6 9 ♗b1!? (9 ♗xa6 ♘xa6 10 ♕e2, intending to castle kingside and aim for e3-e4, is roughly equal after 10...♘c7 11 0-0) 9...♘c6 10 ♘e5 ♕c7 11 f4 (White employs a stonewall pawn formation to lend support to the knight on e5) 11...♘e7 12 ♗h4 ♘g6 13 ♗g5 ♖fe8 14 h4 ♘f8 15 h5 ♘e4? 16 ♗xe4 dxe4 17 ♘xe4 ♗b7 18 ♘f6+! gave White a winning advantage, Astengo-Giuberchio, Imperia 2000.

b) 5...♗xg3 6 hxg3 ♘bd7 7 ♗d3 and now:

b1) 7...c5 8 c3 h6 9 ♘bd2 ♕c7 10 ♕e2 e5 11 ♘xe5 ♘xe5 12 dxe5 ♕xe5 13 ♗b5+! ♗d7 14 ♗xd7+ ♘xd7 15 ♕g4 0-0-0?! (15...♕e6! is necessary when 16 ♕xg7?? 0-0-0 17 c4 d4 leaves White helpless against the threat of ...♖dg8) 16 ♘f3 ♕e6 17 ♕a4 a6 18 b4! and the opening of lines for White's rooks to attack the enemy king gives White a promising game, Heinzel-Stahr, Seebad Heringsdorf 2000.

b2) 7...g6?!, to counter any threats against the pawn on h7, creates new weaknesses on the dark squares around Black's castled king: 8 ♘bd2 b6 9

♕e2 c5 10 c3 c4 11 ♗c2 b5 12 e4 (whenever Black tries to close the queen-side the best reaction is usually to open lines in the centre by this advance) 12...dxe4 13 ♘xe4 ♘xe4 14 ♗xe4 ♖b8 15 d5! ♘c5 (15...exd5 16 ♗xg6+ is good for White) 16 dxe6 ♘xe6? (16...♗xe6 is a better choice but 17 ♗c6+ maintains White's edge) 17 ♗c6+ ♗d7 (17...♔f8 is not possible due to 18 ♕e5 simultaneously attacking both rooks) 18 ♖d1 pinning the bishop and winning the game, Jovanović-Kouznetsov, Paris 2000.

6 ♘bd2 ♘xg3 7 hxg3 ♘d7

7...c5 is a standard way to try and weaken White's central pawns. For instance, 8 c3 ♘c6 9 ♕c2 (White takes advantage of the absence of the king's knight by attacking the pawn on h7 and preparing to castle queenside) 9...g6 10 0-0-0 ♗d7 11 ♗b5 cxd4 12 exd4 ♕f6 13 ♖h6 ♔e7 14 ♗xc6 ♗xc6 15 ♖dh1 when the pressure against the h-pawn gave White the initiative in M.Piket-Van der Werf, Dutch Team Ch 2000.

8 ♗d3

White points the bishop in the direction of the h7 pawn, placing a temporary question mark against Black's usual plan of kingside castling.

8...c6

8...f5 is a logical continuation because it blocks any diagonal threat to h7 and stops White's options of e3-e4. However White can respond sharply by 9 g4! to put Black under pressure. Byway-Merriman, British Team Ch (4NCL) 1996, continued 9...0-0 (if 9...fxg4 then 10 ♘h4 ♘f6 11 ♘g6! ♖g8 12 ♘e5 is in White's favour because Black has been forced to abandon the idea of kingside castling) 10 c4 (White has the easy and straightforward task of undermining Black's central pawns) 10...c6 11 ♕c2 ♕f6 12 gxf5 exf5 13 0-0-0 (once again in this opening White castles queenside in order to exploit the semi-open h-file) 13...g6 14 ♕b3 ♔g7 15 ♖h3 (White strives to keep control of the position and minimise any counterplay. After 15 cxd5 cxd5 16 ♕xd5 ♘b6 17 ♕a5 ♗e6 Black has good piece play for the pawn) 15...a5 16 ♖dh1 (White is relentless in the pursuit of his attack) 16...♖h8

17 cxd5 a4 18 ♕d1 cxd5 19 ♘h4 ♘f8 20 f4 ♗e6 21 ♘df3 a3 22 b3 ♕d8 23 ♘g5 ♗d7 24 ♘xg6! (a clever breakthrough laying bare the black king) 24...♘xg6 25 ♖xh7+ ♖xh7 26 ♖xh7+ ♔g8 27 ♕h5 ♕e8 28 ♔d1 ♗f8 29 ♖xd7 ♕xd7 30 ♕xg6+ ♗g7 31 ♗xf5 1-0.

8...c5 is also a likely move. As usual White should meet it with 9 c3, after which might follow:

a) 9...c4!? 10 ♗xh7? (10 ♗c2, intending e3-e4, gives White a slight edge) 10...♘f8 when the bishop is pinned.

b) 9...e5 10 dxe5 ♘xe5 11 ♘xe5 ♗xe5 12 ♖h5! ♗f6 13 ♕a4+ ♗d7 14 ♗b5 leaves the d5 pawn looking vulnerable.

9 e4 ♕b6

Or 9...dxe4 10 ♘xe4 ♗e7 11 ♕e2, intending to castle queenside, is good for White.

10 e5 ♗e7 11 ♖b1 ♕c7

The grandmaster is satisfied at having ruled out long castling and now retreats, intending to fianchetto on the queenside.

12 c3 b6 13 0-0 ♗b7 14 b4

White's strategy is to restrict Black by queenside expansion.

14...a5 15 b5 0-0 16 ♕e2 ♖fc8 17 a4 ♕d8

If 17...cxb5 then 18 ♗xb5 ♘f8 19 ♖fc1 gives White a slight edge.

18 ♖fc1 ♖c7

19 c4

In order to enable his pieces to exert greater influence on the queenside White needs either to create pawn weaknesses or open up the position.

19...c5 20 cxd5 ♗xd5 21 ♗e4 ♘f8 22 ♘c4 cxd4

22...♖d7!? is also possible to defend the b6 pawn with the queen.

23 ♘xd4 ♗c5 24 ♘c6 ♕g5 25 ♘d2

The possession of extra space allows Kocovski to improve the position of his pieces with ease. The knight is heading for b3, aiming to exchange the active bishop on c5.

25...♘g6

Not 25...♕xg3? which is busted by 26 ♖xc5 breaking the pin on the f-pawn and winning easily.

26 ♗xd5 exd5 27 ♘b3 ♗f8 28 ♖d1

White's trumps are the influential knight on c6 and the long-term weakness of the d5 pawn.

28...♘e7 29 ♘bd4 ♖e8 30 ♖b3 ♘g6? 31 f4!

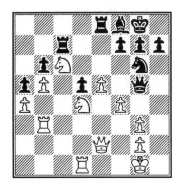

The white knights make a great team and not only deny the black queen squares of retreat but also help to capture her.

31...♕h6 32 ♘f5 ♗c5+ 33 ♘cd4 1-0

The idea of playing ...c7-c5, to challenge the centre and allow Black to harass the b2 pawn with ...♕b6, is a critical line in the London System.

Bai-Bagoly
Aggtelek Cseppko 1998

1 d4 d5 2 ♘f3 ♘f6 3 ♗f4 e6 4 e3 c5

Black intends to apply some pressure on White's central pawns.

5 c3 ♘c6 6 ♘bd2

6...♕b6

With the bishop on f4 the black queen targets the unprotected pawn on b2. Also possible is 6...♘h5 with the obvious intention of exchanging pieces. Dgebuadze-Savchenko, Ubeda 1998, saw 7 ♗g5 ♕b6 (7...♗e7 8 ♗xe7 ♕xe7 9 ♗d3 is about equal although the knight is not well placed) 8 dxc5 ♗xc5 (the tempting 8...♕xb2?! runs into 9 ♘d4!, threatening the knight on h5, when 9...♘f6 10 ♘b5 ♔d8 11 ♗c4!, intending ♖b1, traps the black queen) 9 b4 ♗e7 10 b5 ♘b8 (Black must forfeit the right to castle since 10...♗xg5? 11 ♘xg5 uncovers an attack against the knight on h5 and secures a big advantage) 11 ♗xe7 ♔xe7 12 c4 ♘f6 13 cxd5 exd5 (if 13...♘xd5 then the lack of control over the c4 square allows White to step up the pressure with 14 e4 ♘f6 15 ♘c4 ♕c5 16 e5 ♘d5 17 ♖c1 ♕b4+ 18 ♘fd2 with a clear plus due to the vulnerable black king) 14 ♗e2 ♗e6 15 a4 ♕d6 16 0-0 (White has completed his development whereas Black's king hampers the rest of his pieces) 16...♘bd7 17 ♕b1 ♖hc8 18 ♕b2 ♘b6 19 ♘d4 ♔f8 20 a5 led to an advantage for White.

A more challenging line is 6...cxd4 7 exd4 when 7...♗d6 is similar to play in the main game Kocovski-Mitkov. For instance:

a) 8 ♗g3 ♕c7 9 ♗d3 0-0 10 ♕e2 ♘d7 11 ♘g5 (perhaps 11 0-0!? should be played) 11...♘f6 12 ♘gf3 ♘d7 13 0-0 ♗xg3 14 hxg3 e5 15 ♘xe5 ♘dxe5 16 dxe5 ♘xe5 17 ♘f3 ♖e8 18 ♘xe5 ♖xe5 19 ♕d2 with a small advantage to White due to the weakness of the isolated d-pawn, Van de Mortel-Jongsma, Haarlem 2001.

b) 8 ♘e5 is essentially the best way to avoid an early exchange of dark-squared bishops: 8...♕c7 9 ♗b5 0-0 10 ♕e2 a6 11 ♗d3 b5 12 a3 ♗b7 13 0-0 with an edge, Barton-Tidman, Southend 1999.

7 ♖b1

The rook defends the b-pawn and is handily placed for a queenside pawn advance. Instead 7 ♕b1 has been tried as an elaborate way of looking after the b2 pawn and exerting control over the e4 square. I just think it is easier to stick to the plan of developing the kingside by ♗d3, followed by 0-0 and ♘e5 to transfer the queen to the kingside. It might be a familiar theme but against slightly inaccurate defence it can work wonders.

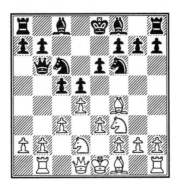

7...♗d7

The text usually transposes to other lines but it can have independent value if Black wants to get his queen's rook quickly involved in the action. Also possible:

a) 7...♗e7 8 ♗d3 (as usual White adopts the standard set-up of preparing 0-0 followed by ♘e5 to allow the queen to join in the attack) 8...♗d7 9 0-0 0-0 10 ♘e5 ♖fd8 11 ♕f3 ♘xe5 12 dxe5 ♘e4 (after 12...♘e8 13 ♕h5 h6 14 ♕g4 maintains the initiative) 13 ♘xe4 dxe4 14 ♗xe4 ♖ab8 15 ♖fd1 when the extra pawn gave White a clear advantage in Hebden-Psakhis, Isle of Man 1999.

b) 7...g6 is playable but generally frowned upon because Black has already moved his e-pawn and so will find his dark squares weakened when his bishop emerges on g7. 8 ♗d3 ♗g7 9 h3 ♘d7!? (an interesting idea to use the bishop on g7 to generate support for advancing the e-pawn) 10 ♗h2 0-0 11 0-0 e5 12 dxc5 ♘xc5 13 ♗c2 ♗e6 14 b4 ♘e4 (or 14...♘d7 15 ♘g5 is roughly equal) 15 ♘xe4 dxe4 16 ♘d2 ♗xa2 17 ♖a1 ♗e6 18 ♗b3 ♗xb3 19 ♕xb3 a5 20 ♘xe4 axb4 21 ♖ab1! with equal chances, Miles-Turner, British Ch 2000.

c) 7...♘h5 8 ♗g5 h6 9 ♗h4 cxd4 (9...g5 walks into 10 ♘e5! allowing White an edge) 10 ♘xd4 (rejecting 10 exd4 on the basis that the f4 square will then be available for Black's knight) 10...♘xd4 11 cxd4 with equal chances, Szabolcsi-Bellon Lopez, French Team Ch 2000.

8 ♗d3 cxd4

Black wants to rule out any possibility of dxc5 followed by b2-b4 but exchanging pawns introduces another problem.

9 exd4

It seems that the position has not changed much but in fact White has gained a positional plus in that his knight on e5 can now be supported by a rook or queen along the e-file. The difference, compared to the note on 6...cxd4 in the game Van de Mortel-Jongsma, Haarlem 2001, is that Black cannot contest his opponent's dominance of the important e5 square by ...♗d6.

9...♖c8 10 0-0 ♘a5

Bagoly has achieved his short-term goal of placing a rook on the c-file and has the possibility of ♘c4. However he has neglected his kingside development and White can progress with the standard plan.

11 ♕e2 ♗e7 12 ♘e5

The knight comes to e5, which should be a familiar sight to anyone who plays this opening. It stops ...♘c4 and opens the d1-h5 diagonal for the white queen.

12...0-0 13 ♗g5

Of course the simple threat is 14 ♗xf6 followed by 15 ♘xd7.

13...♕c7 14 f4

The f-pawn supports the knight on e5 and more importantly introduces the idea of ♖f3-h3 to bolster the attack. With a closed centre, signs of queenside counterplay from Black are a long way off.

14...♗d6?

Bagoly wants to get rid of the strong e5 knight but this is the wrong way to do it. 14...♘c6 might be an admission that the opening has gone wrong but at least it keeps Black in the game.

15 ♗xf6 gxf6 16 ♕g4+ ♔h8 17 ♕h4! 1-0

The timing of ...c7-c5 is important. For example, if this advance is made after only three moves, White has an extra option available.

Kahn-I.Almasi

Hungarian Championship 2000

1 d4 d5 2 ♘f3 ♘f6 3 ♗f4 c5

The swift advance of the c-pawn is regarded as one of the main defences to the London System.

4 dxc5!?

A number of ideas have been tried to prevent Black from equalising and this capture is an obvious option. The simple idea is to hang on to the extra pawn and exploit the material advantage in some way. An obvious drawback is that White concedes the centre and Black can accelerate his development by fighting to win back the pawn. The alternatives 4 c3 or 4 e3 are discussed in the rest of the chapter.

4...e6 5 b4

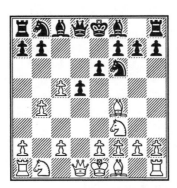

If White does not defend the pawn then why bother taking on c5?

5...♘c6

Black brings the knight into the game and attacks the b4 pawn. 5...a5 is the direct response to undermine the protection of the c5-pawn. After 6 c3 play might continue:

a) 6...axb4 and now:

a1) 7 ♗xb8 is an in-between move that is worth noting:

a1a) 7...♖xb8 8 cxb4 ♖a8 9 e3 b6? (9...♗d7!? should be considered) 10 ♗b5+ ♗d7 11 c6 led to a winning advantage in Lewandowicz-Wurst, Bernkastel-Kues 1995.

a1b) 7...b3 8 ♕xb3 ♖xb8 9 c6 ♗d6 10 cxb7 ♖xb7 11 ♕c2 ♗d7 12 ♘bd2 0-0 13 e3 ♕a5 14 ♘b3 ♖xb3! (a nice exchange sacrifice which aims to exploit his lead in development to chase the white queen) 15 ♕xb3 ♖b8 16 ♕c2 ♖c8 17 ♗d3 (or 17 ♘d2 ♖xc3 18 ♕b2 ♘e4 19 ♘xe4 ♖xe3+ 20 ♔d1 ♗a4+ winning) 17...♖xc3 18 ♕d2 ♗b5! 19 0-0 (19 ♗xb5? allows a pretty combination after 19...♘e4 20 ♕e2? ♖c1 mate) 19...♗xd3 led to a winning advantage in Tobak-Sumets, Odessa 2000.

a2) 7 cxb4?! ♘c6 8 ♘c3 (White decides not to bother trying to hang on to the extra material and prefers to get his pieces out) 8...♘xb4 9 ♘b5 ♘a6 10 ♘d6+ ♗xd6 11 ♗xd6 (11 cxd6 ♘e4 12 ♖c1) 11...♘xc5! 12 ♗e5 (unfortunately for White 12 ♗xc5 does not win a piece due to 12...♕a5+ 13 ♕d2 ♕xc5 when Black remains a pawn up) 12...0-0 13 e3 ♘fe4 and the extra pawn gives Black a winning advantage, Orso-Gonzalez Garcia, Budapest 1998.

b) 6...♗d7 7 ♘bd2 b6! 8 cxb6 axb4 9 cxb4 ♗xb4 10 ♗c7 ♕c8 11 ♕b3 ♘c6 12 a3 (12 e3 ♖a3 13 ♕b2 ♕a8 with double-edged play) 12...0-0 13 ♕b2 ♗e7!? 14 b7 ♕xc7 15 bxa8=♕ ♖xa8 (Black is the exchange down but has plenty of compensation due to his active pieces) 16 e3 ♘e4 17 ♕c2 ♗f6 18 ♖c1 (18 ♖b1 ♕a5 19 ♗d3 ♘xd2 20 ♘xd2 ♘e5 with the initiative) 18...♖xa3 19 ♘xe4 (19 ♗e2, to try and mobilise the kingside, is shown to be too slow after 19...♖c3 20 ♕b1 ♘d4) 19...dxe4 20 ♕xe4 (20 ♘d2 ♖c3 21 ♕xc3 ♗xc3 22 ♖xc3 has been suggested but 22...♕a5 looks good for Black) 20...♕a5+ 21 ♘d2 ♗c3 (it is significant that the crisis facing White is due to his lack of development which has resulted in his king being stuck in the centre of the board) 22 ♕d3 ♘e5 23 ♕d6 g6 (Black is wary of a back rank mate) 24 ♖b1 ♖a1 25 ♕b8+ ♔g7 26 ♖xa1 ♕xa1+ 27 ♔e2 ♕a2 28 ♕d6 ♗b5+ 29 ♔d1 ♕a1+ 30 ♔c2 ♗a4+ 0-1 Crouch-Yakovich, Port Erin 2001.

6 c3 a5 7 ♘d4

7 b5 ♘a7 8 e3 ♗xc5 is fine for Black who gets his pawn back and has the better pawn structure.

7...axb4 8 ♘xc6 bxc6 9 cxb4 ♘e4

10 ♗e5?!

To cover the weakened long a1-h8 diagonal but better seems 10 e3!? ♗e7 (10...♕f6 is easily rebuffed by 11 ♕d4) 11 ♘d2 ♗f6 (the alternative 11...♘xd2 12 ♕xd2 ♗f6 is designed to exploit the dark squares after 13 ♖d1 e5 14 ♗g3 0-0 when Black has some compensation for the pawn based on the central pawns and pressure on the a-file.) 12 ♘xe4 ♗xa1 13 ♘d6+ ♔f8 14 ♕xa1 etc

10...♕g5 11 ♗d4

11 ♗b2 runs into 11...♕f4 12 ♕d4 ♖a4! 13 a3 ♗xc5 winning.

11...e5 12 ♗e3 ♕f6

Black is spoilt for choice since 12...♕h4 13 ♕c1 d4 is also better for Black.

13 ♘d2 ♘c3 14 ♕c1

If 14 ♕c2 then 14...d4 15 ♘f3 ♗f5 is fine for Black.

14...d4

A precise response because the combination 14...♘xa2 15 ♕b2 d4 16 ♗xd4 exd4 17 ♖xa2 ♖xa2 18 ♕xa2 gives White a slight edge.

15 ♘f3 ♘xa2!

There is no rush to take the bishop so Black grabs a pawn. Instead, 15...dxe3 16 ♕xc3 exf2+ 17 ♔xf2 gives White a chance to survive.

16 ♕b2 dxe3 17 ♖xa2 ♖xa2 18 ♕xa2 e4 19 ♕a8

Kahn hopes that Black will play ...exf3 so he can take the bishop and have at least perpetual check.

19...♕c3+ 20 ♔d1 ♕b3+ 21 ♔c1 ♕c4+ 22 ♔d1 ♕d5+ 23 ♔c1 ♔d7

This looks a bit odd but an exceptional position has been reached. Indeed it makes a lot of sense defending with the king rather than the queen because this enables him to maintain his strong initiative.

24 ♕a7+ ♔e6 25 ♕c7

25 ♕a3 is probably the best way to keep the game going but after 25...♕c4+ 26 ♔b2 exf3 27 ♕xe3+ ♔d7 28 ♕d2+ ♔c7 29 exf3 White has little to show for the piece.

25...♗e7 26 ♘d4+ ♕xd4 27 ♕xc6+ ♔e5 28 ♕c7+ ♔f6 29 ♕f4+ ♗f5 30 g4 0-1

In the next game White cements his d4 pawn by 4 e3 and then invites complications with the daring 5 ♘c3 offering to gambit a pawn.

Mastrapa-Medina

Havana 2000

1 d4 d5 2 ♘f3 ♘f6 3 ♗f4 c5 4 e3 ♕b6

The queen pops out to attack b2 in a bid to exploit the f4-bishop's absence from the queenside. Whether it is an improvement on the normal continuation 4...♘c6 is debatable, but it does have the advantage of avoiding lines associated with ♕b3 or ♕c2 after the white c-pawn has moved.

5 ♘c3!?

Obviously White is careful when sacrificing a pawn and in this instance the text sets a trap that has claimed a number of victims: 5...♕xb2? fails to 6 ♘b5 ♘a6 7 ♖b1 ♕xa2 8 ♖a1 ♕b2 9 ♖xa6! bxa6 10 ♘c7+ winning.

It is also possible to protect the pawn with the solid 5 ♕c1. For example:

a) 5...♘c6 6 c3 ♗f5 and now White has two main ideas:

a1) 7 ♘bd2 cxd4 (or 7...e6 8 ♘h4 ♗g4 9 ♗d3 with a small edge) 8 exd4 ♖c8 9 a3 h6 10 ♗e2 g5 11 ♗e3 ♗g7 12 ♘e5 with equal chances, Sturua-Salem, Dubai 2002.

a2) 7 ♘h4 ♗d7 8 ♘d2 cxd4 9 exd4 ♖c8 10 ♕b1 (10 ♗d3? allows 10...♘xd4 taking advantage of the pin on the c-file) 10...e6 11 ♘hf3 ♘a5 12 a4 ♘b3 13 ♘xb3 ♕xb3 14 ♗d3 ♕b6 15 ♘e5 ♗e7 16 0-0 ♗c6 17 a5 ♕d8 18 ♘xc6 ♖xc6 19 ♗b5 led to victory in Kovacević-Castillo Gallego, Mancha Real 2000.

5...a6

Black understandably wishes to stop the possibility of ♘b5. This can also be achieved by other moves:

a) 5...c4 (the standard recommendation to stop White from placing the white-squared bishop on d3) 6 ♖b1 e6 7 a3 (a refinement to stop ...♗b4) 7...♗d6 8 ♗xd6 ♕xd6 9 ♘e5 ♘bd7 10 f4 (the stonewall pawn formation secures the knight in the centre) 10...a6 11 ♗e2 b5 12 ♗f3 ♗b7 13 0-0 0-0 14 ♕e1 ♘b6 15 g4! (with the centre closed White is happy to advance the pawns in front of his king) 15...♕e7 16 ♕h4 ♘c8 17 g5 (White acts quickly otherwise Black will play ...♘c8-d6 to support a knight on e4) 17...♘e4 18 ♗xe4 dxe4 19 f5 exf5 20 ♖xf5 ♘d6 21 ♖f4 f5 22 gxf6 ½-½ M.Piket-Rogozenko, Dutch Team Ch 2001.

b) 5 ...♗d7 (the bishop covers the b5 square to ward off the white knight) 6 ♖b1 e6 7 ♗e2 ♗e7 8 0-0 0-0 9 a3 a5 10 ♖e1 ♗c6 11 ♘e5 ♘bd7 12 ♗d3 ♖ac8 13 ♘xc6 ♖xc6 14 ♕f3 (after shuffling his pieces around the board, White goes on the attack) 14...♖d8 15 ♕h3 cxd4 16 exd4 ♕xd4 17 ♗g5 (the threat is ♗xh7+) 17...g6?! (17...h6!? is a sterner test of the sacrifice) 18 ♖bd1 ♕a7 19 ♗b5 ♖cc8 20 ♖xe6 fxe6 21 ♕xe6+ ♔f8 22 ♗h6+ ♔e8 23 ♘xd5 1-0 Ehrke-Stam, Gausdal 1998.

6 ♘a4

I quite like the idea of 6 a3, once again setting a trap as 6...♕xb2?? walks into the sneaky 7 ♘a4 winning. Instead, Kovacević-Kuljasević, Pula 2002, continued 6...cxd4 7 exd4 ♘c6 8 h3 ♗f5 9 ♘a4 ♕d8 10 ♘c5 with roughly equal chances.

6...♕a5+ 7 c3

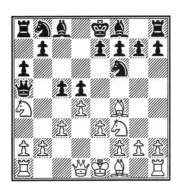

7...cxd4!?

Though it seems perfectly natural to take on d4, the text has proved harmless for White. This is because the semi-open e-file will allow White to lend extra support to a knight on e5 and it is easy to develop a bishop to the active d3 square. Moreover it is only a matter of time before White threatens b2-b4, gaining space while attacking the queen.

Also possible:

a) 7...c4 (preventing the ideal development of the bishop on d3) 8 b4 ♕d8 9 ♘e5 (9 ♕c2 g6 10 ♗e2 ♗g7 11 0-0 0-0 12 ♘d2 is level) 9... ♘bd7 10 ♗e2 g6 11 g4 ♗g7 12 h4 h5 13 g5 ♘e4 14 f3 ♘d6 15 ♘c5 with a double-edged position, Lueders-Wellendorf, Berlin 2000.

b) 7...♘bd7 8 ♘xc5 ♘xc5 9 b4 (9 dxc5 ♕xc5 10 ♗d3 is also possible) 9...♕a3 10 bxc5 ♕xc3+ 11 ♘d2 ♘e4 12 ♖c1 ♕xd2+ 13 ♕xd2 ♘xd2 14 ♔xd2 gives White a comfortable ending due to his space advantage.

8 exd4 e6 9 b4 ♕d8 10 ♗d3

White takes steps to catch up with development. As usual in the London System the light-squared bishop comes to d3, a knight goes to e5 and White castles kingside.

10...♗d6 11 ♘e5 ♕c7 12 0-0 ♘c6 13 ♖e1

After the exchange on d4, White has the advantage of the semi-open e-file which allows him to reinforce his knight on e5 with the king's rook.

13...b6 14 ♗g3 ♗b7 15 f4

White creates a sort of stonewall pawn formation to consolidate the knight on e5—although 15 ♕f3 also deserves consideration.

15...♘e4?

At first glance it seems to be a good idea to install a knight on e4 to ward off White's attack—but it does not work. Therefore 15...0-0!? should be considered.

16 ♗xe4 dxe4 17 ♘c4!

It is important that White does not rush things because 17 ♖xe4 ♘xb4 would be fine for Black.

17...♗xf4

Black is in trouble as the obvious 17...b5 allows 18 ♘xd6+ ♕xd6 19 ♘c5 ♘d8 20 f5 with a tremendous attack.

18 ♗xf4 ♕xf4 19 ♖xe4! ♕c7

Medina has little choice considering that the pawn is taboo because of 19...♕xe4? 20 ♘d6+ and the black queen will leave the board.

20 ♘axb6 ♖d8 21 d5! 0-0

What else?

Black will not gain much encouragement from 21...♘a7 22 ♕d4 0-0 23 d6 ♕c6 24 ♖g4 (spot the threat!) 24...g6 25 ♘a5 ♕xd6 26 ♘xb7 with a winning advantage.

22 d6 ♕b8

This position is embarrassing for Black because the black queen is locked out of the game which allows White to go on the rampage. The game concluded:

23 ♖h4 ♕a7 24 ♕h5 h6 25 ♕c5 f5 26 a4 f4 27 ♕f2 f3 28 g3 ♖f5 29 ♖e1 ♖f6 30 ♖he4 e5 31 ♘d5 ♖fxd6 32 ♘xd6 ♖xd6 33 ♕xa7 ♘xa7 34 c4 ♘c6 35 ♔f2 ♔h7 36 ♔xf3 ♖d7 37 ♔f2 ♘d4 38 ♖xe5 ♖f7+ 39 ♘f4 ♖f6 40 ♖e7 1-0

Once again White's reaction to 3...c5 is put to the test and 6 ♕c2 proves itself worthy of further investigation.

Wirthensohn-Plesec

Swiss Team Championship 2002

1 d4 d5 2 ♗f4 ♘f6 3 e3 c5 4 c3 ♘c6 5 ♘f3 ♕b6

6 ♕c2!?

The queen protects the b-pawn. I think this is a good recommendation because the main alternatives 6 ♕b3 and 6 ♕c1 are well known and won't force the average player to stop and think. The little known 6 ♘a3 might also be worth a try. For instance:

a) 6...♕xb2 7 ♘b5 ♘e4, threatening mate on f2, when White might continue:

a1) 8 ♗g3 ♔d8 9 dxc5 (White can take a draw if he wants with 9 ♖b1 ♕xa2 10 ♖a1 ♕b2 11 ♖b1 and the black queen cannot avoid perpetual attack) 9...♘xc3 (9...e6 10 ♖b1 ♕xa2 11 ♗d3 is unclear) 10 ♘xc3 ♕xc3+ 11 ♘d2 is unclear according to an analysis by Kaidanov.

a2) 8 ♘d2? ♘xc3 9 ♘c7+ ♔d8 10 ♕c1 ♕xc1+ 11 ♖xc1 ♘xa2 12 ♖a1 ♘ab4 13 ♘xa8 ♘c2+ 14 ♔d1 ♘xa1 when White can give up, Orlov-Milenković, Cetinje 1990.

b) 6...a6 7 ♕b3 and now:

b1) 7...♕xb3 8 axb3, intending ♘b5 to take advantage of the pin on the a-file, is better for White.

b2) 7...♕a5 8 dxc5 e6 9 ♗e2 ♗xc5 10 0-0 0-0 11 c4 d4 12 exd4 ♘xd4 13 ♘xd4 ♗xd4 14 ♘c2 ♗e5 15 ♗xe5 (15 ♗e3 ♗d7 is level according to Kaidanov) 15...♕xe5 with equal chances, Miles-Kaidanov, Chicago 2000.

b3) 7...♕a7 8 dxc5 e6 (8...♕xc5 9 ♗d3 followed by kingside castling gives White an edge) 9 ♗d6 ♗xd6 10 cxd6 0-0 11 ♗e2 ♖d8 12 0-0 ♖xd6 (Black regains the pawn but still needs to co-ordinate his pieces) 13 c4 ♘a5 14 ♕b4 ♕b6 15 ♕xb6 ♖xb6 16 b3 dxc4 17 ♘xc4 ♘xc4 18 ♗xc4 ♗d7 19 ♖fd1 ♗b5 20 ♖ac1 g6 ½-½ Nielsen-Akesson, Copenhagen 2001.

c) 6...c4 7 ♕c1 ♗f5 8 ♘h4 ♗g6 9 ♗e2 e6 10 0-0 with equal chances, Astengo-Farina, Limone Piemonte 2001.

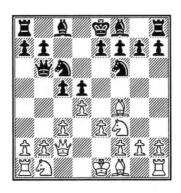

6...♗f5?!

Anyone who has a flair for tactics will be tempted by this move because if the bishop is taken then Black simply plays 7...♕xb2 winning material.

The only problem is that there is a decent in-between move available for White. Other moves are:

a) 6...♗g4 7 dxc5 (or 7 ♘e5 ♘xe5 8 dxe5 ♘d7 9 c4 d4 10 exd4 cxd4 11 ♘d2 g6 12 ♕b3 when the players decided to take a rest, ½-½ Miles-Fressinet, Mondariz 2000) 7...♕xc5 8 ♘e5 ♘xe5 9 ♗xe5 ♘d7 10 ♗g3 g6 11 ♕a4 ♗f5 12 ♘d2 ♗g7 13 ♗e2 0-0 14 ♘b3 ♕b6 15 0-0 is roughly equal, Wirthensohn-Giertz, Swiss Team Ch 2001.

b) 6...c4 7 ♘bd2 (whenever Black tries to close the position on the queenside then White tends to prepare the liberating e3-e4) 7...♘h5 8 ♗e5 f6 9 ♗g3 ♘xg3 10 hxg3 f5?! (Black is still worried about the prospect of e3-e4) 11 ♘h4! ♘d8 12 ♘xf5 ♕g6 13 g4 (13 e4 is also good news for White after 13...dxe4 14 ♘e3 b5 15 ♗e2) 13...♕xg4 14 ♘g3 g6 15 e4 gave White a lead in development and the better pawn structure in Loyer-Duchene, Montlucon 1997.

7 dxc5! ♗xc2 8 cxb6 ♗xb1

Or 8...axb6 9 ♘a3 (intending ♘b5) 9...♗e4 10 ♘b5 ♖a5 (10...0-0-0 11 ♘e5 ♘xe5 12 ♗xe5 with a good game) 11 b4 ♖a4 12 ♗e2 ♔d7 13 0-0 e6 14 ♘e5+ ♘xe5 15 ♗xe5 ♗e7 16 ♘d4 when the threat of ♗b5+ gave White the superior chances in Astengo-Ruzzier, Bozen 1998.

9 ♖xb1 axb6

The doubled b-pawns are a long-term weakness although this is compensated by the semi-open a-file.

10 ♗b5!

10...♖xa2?!

A natural move which few could resist. Plesec has gained a pawn but at the cost of neglecting his development and White is hoping that his active pieces will create serious threats. A modest improvement is 10...e6 to help activate the kingside pieces.

11 0-0 e6 12 ♖a1 ♜a5

Grabbing further material by 12...♜xb2 allows White to mobilise his pieces to attack the black king after 13 ♖a8+ ♚e7 14 ♗xc6 bxc6 15 ♖fa1 ♘d7 (if 15...e5 then 16 ♘xe5 c5 17 ♖1a7+ ♚e6 18 g4 is good for White) 16 ♘e5 g5 17 ♗xg5+ f6 18 f4 when I prefer White's chances.

13 ♘d4 ♚d7 14 ♗xc6+ bxc6 15 b4!

The rook on a5 stops White from invading the heart of Black's position so it is persuaded to leave by the pawn attack.

15...♜xa1 16 ♖xa1 c5

An attempt to get the king's rook into the game with 16...♗e7 fails to 17 ♖a7+ ♚e8 18 ♘xc6 winning.

17 ♖a7+ ♚e8 18 ♘c6

White is well placed to dominate the position and it is clear that the pawn deficit is a mere detail.

18...♘e4

It is difficult for Black to find constructive moves. The alternative 18...cxb4 19 cxb4 achieves little. For instance: 19...♖g8 20 b5 (the position is so good that 20 ♖a8+ is also strong: 20...♚d7 21 ♘e5+ ♚e7 22 b5 leaves Black tied up and with his b6 pawn about to fall—after which White will have a winning advantage due to his passed b5 pawn) 20...♗c5 21 ♗g5 (threatening ♗xf6 and then ♖a8+) 21...♖f8 22 ♘e5 ♗e7 23 ♘d7! ♘xd7 24 ♖a8+ ♘b8 25 ♖xb8+ ♚d7 26 ♖b7+ and Black can resign.

19 ♖a8+ ♚d7 20 b5

20...e5

Black hands back a pawn to avoid the ignominy of ♖d8 mate.

21 ♗xe5 f6 22 f3! ♘d2

Or 22...fxe5 23 fxe4 dxe4 24 ♘xe5+ (White is effectively playing with a couple of extra pieces) 24...♔e6 25 ♖e8+ ♔d5 26 c4+ ♔d6 27 ♘f7+ ♔d7 28 ♖b8 ♖g8 29 ♘g5 ♖h8 30 ♖xb6 winning.

23 ♗g3 ♘c4 24 e4 dxe4 25 fxe4 g6

At first glance 25...♘d6, to fork the b and e-pawn, seems fine but it is of little use after 26 ♖a7+ ♔e8 (26...♔e6 27 ♘d8 mate) 27 ♗xd6 ♗xd6 28 ♖a8+ when Black is busted.

26 ♖a4 ♘d2

If 26...♘d6 then 27 ♖a7+ is similar to the analysis in the note to move 25.

27 ♖a7+ ♔e8

27...♔e6 28 ♘d8 mate.

28 e5 fxe5 29 ♘xe5 c4 30 ♗f2 ♘e4 31 ♗d4 ♖g8

Finally the rook makes a move—a fitting tribute to White's python-like grip on the game.

32 ♘xc4 1-0

SUMMARY

The standard set-up of pieces in the London System is on show in the game **Tseitlin-Liesmann**. White reacts quickly to the prospect of a kingside attack by installing a knight on the e5 square and transferring the queen to the kingside. A model example of how creative handling of the opening makes it a case of White to play and win! The dark-squared bishop is important to White but the fact that he can survive and prosper even if it is exchanged is shown by the game **Kocovski-Mitkov**. The first example of Black trying to exploit the early excursion of White's bishop to f4 by playing ...♕b6 is discussed in **Bai-Bagoly**. White simply carries on developing in accepted fashion and Black runs out of decent ideas. It is worth remembering 14 f4 because this way of supporting the knight on e5 allows the king's rook to enter the fray via f3. If Black plays 3...c5 why not take the pawn? This idea is explored in **Kahn-I.Almasi** and it Black who emerges on top thanks to his rapid development while White is trying to hang on to the extra pawn. It is easier for White to support the centre with 4 e3 and then worry about 4...♕b6. **Mastrapa-Medina** sees the marvellous 5 ♘c3, which invites Black to go wrong by greedily grabbing pawns. **Wirthensohn-Plesec** sees 4 c3 and White protecting his b2-pawn with the queen. Black tries to play aggressively but it backfires and White conducts a tactical ending superbly. The London System is clearly a reliable opening with plenty of opportunities for a kingside attack.

THE CHIGORIN

The Chigorin is a good surprise weapon against the Queen's Gambit and has a legion of dedicated followers. The drawback is that after 2 ♘f3 Black needs to continue 2...♘c6 and wait expectantly for c2-c4 if the Chigorin is his main weapon against 1 d4. But the good news for followers of the London System is that c2-c4 can be delayed long enough to steer the game away from traditional paths, thereby forcing Black into unknown territory.

HISTORY OF THE CHIGORIN

The brilliant Russian chess pioneer Mikhail Ivanovich Chigorin (1850-1908) made some great contributions to opening theory. The defence that bears his name occurs after 1 d4 d5 2 c4 ♘c6 and is primarily designed as an anti-Queen's Gambit weapon. It has been a favourite of club players for years because there are relatively few variations to memorize. Although top players have traditionally rejected the idea of blocking their c-pawn with the queen's knight and preferred other methods of challenging the centre, the Chigorin tradition has been revived in recent years with Russia's Alexander Morozevich championing it successfully at the highest level.

IDEAS BEHIND THE OPENING

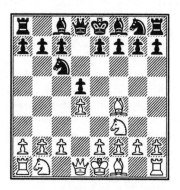

The London System is ideally suited to meet the Chigorin Defence because the omission of an early c2-c4 by White cancels out numerous tricky variations. Instead, most Black players meet 2 ♘f3 with 2...♘c6, assuming that the game will soon transpose after a future c2-c4. But, faced with a London player they will be disappointed. And so they find themselves in a fight for the e5 square and in some cases even manage to play an appropriate ...e7-e5.

HOW TO BEAT THE CHIGORIN

I think the key to frustrating Chigorin players is to omit c2-c4 which merely allows them to get back to familiar territory. With a knight on c6, one idea for Black is to play for ...e7-e5, but against this the London formation of a knight on f3 and bishop on f4 is particularly effective. The usual principles of rapid development and a solid pawn structure are a good basis for success. There have been a couple of recent, good books on the opening, *The Chigorin Queen's Gambit* by Angus Dunnington and *Unusual Queen's Gambit Declined* by Chris Ward, so it is good to know what they advocate against the move-order I am proposing. Dunnington understandably concentrates on the main lines and briefly mentions the line, suggesting that c2-c4 will probably be played sooner or later anyway, but if not then Black should just continue developing his pieces. He might have a point but it won't be much help if Black is trying to look up an antidote to the London System. Chris Ward goes one step better by publishing one of his victories as White but offers no decent alternatives for Black.

The first example shows what can happen if White sticks to the basic London System plan against a casual defence.

Grube-Zawierta
Hagenbach 1998

1 d4 d5 2 ♘f3 ♘c6 3 ♗f4 ♘f6

Black gets on with the job of developing. The main alternatives, 3...♗f5 and ♗g4, are explored later in the chapter.

4 e3

4...e6

Black voluntarily blocks in his light-squared bishop, which is a tame way to handle the opening especially when ...c7-c5 is not available to open the position.

Others:

a) 4...♘h5 (it is too early in the opening to waste time chasing the bishop) 5 ♗g5 h6 6 ♗h4 ♕d6 (or 6...g5 7 ♗g3 ♘xg3 8 hxg3 ♗g7 9 c4 giving White a slight plus) 7 ♘fd2 ♘f6 8 ♗g3 ♕b4?! 9 b3 ♕a5 (Black is second best here because moving the queen so much results in neglected development of his other pieces) 10 c3 ♗f5 11 b4 ♕b6 12 a4 a5 13 b5 ♘b8 14 c4 c5 15 bxc6 ♕xc6 16 cxd5 ♕xd5 17 ♘c3 ♕e6 18 ♗c4 ♕c8 19 ♘b5 and White had a clear advantage in Markopoulos-Papakanellos, Patras 2001.

b) 4...a6 is seen surprisingly regularly but it is geared to lines where White makes a quick advance of the c-pawn. For instance: 5 c4 ♗f5 6 ♘c3 e6 7 ♖c1 ♘e4 8 ♘xe4 ♗xe4 9 ♘d2 ♗b4 10 a3 ♗xd2+ 11 ♕xd2 0-0 12 f3 with equal chances, Kacheishvili-Lindfeldt, Golden Sands 2000.

5 ♗d3

Directing the bishop towards the kingside in preparation for an attack. White has plenty of options at this stage:

a) 5 ♘bd2 ♗e7 6 h3 (to allow the bishop to retreat if Black tries to exchange it by ...♘h5) 6...a6 7 a4 ♗d7 8 c3 ♘e4 9 ♘xe4 (9 ♗d3!?) 9...dxe4 10 ♘d2 f5 11 a5 (White is content to stake a claim for a space advantage) 11...♗f6 12 ♘c4 ♗c8 13 ♗e2 0-0 14 0-0 with a slight edge, Kovacević-Zemerov, Harkany 1994.

b) 5 c4 (Black's set-up is rather meek so there is a case for advancing the c-pawn early) 5...♗e7 6 ♘c3 0-0 7 ♖c1 a6 8 a3 ♘a7 9 b4 dxc4 10 ♗xc4 b5 11 ♗d3 c6 12 0-0 ♗b7 13 ♘e4 when White has greater space and superior piece co-ordination, Taimanov-Hardstam, Osterskan 1994.

5...♗d7 6 c3

As usual White relies on a solid pawn structure as a basis for later middle-game prosperity.

6...♗e7 7 h3 0-0 8 ♘bd2

Grube has done nothing more than carry out the standard plan of development—yet already he has an edge. Black's pieces are rather confined and without any immediate prospect of the freeing pawn advance ...c7-c5 or even ...e7-e5 his prospects are bleak.

8...♘h5?!

A pointless move when White has already reserved a square of retreat for his bishop by 7 h3.

9 ♗h2 ♘f6 10 0-0 ♗d6 11 ♘e5

The knight is well placed on e5 where it does a good job of stopping Black from mobilising his pieces.

11...♗e8 12 ♖c1

12 f4 is worthy of investigation since the stonewall pawn formation helps to support the knight on e5. And if Black exchanges the knight then after 13 fxe5 White's king's rook enters the attack.

12...a6 13 ♗b1

The idea is to play ♕c2 and then try to compromise the black kingside by playing ♘g4, exchanging off the defender of the h7 pawn.

13...♘d7 14 f4

If 14 ♕c2 then 14...f5 blocks the diagonal.

14...f6 15 ♘xd7 ♗xd7 16 e4 ♖e8?

An indecisive move at a time when a wait and see policy is not advisable. 16...f5 would at least slow down White's momentum.

17 e5 ♗e7 18 exf6 ♗xf6

18...gxf6 19 ♕h5 f5 20 ♖f3 also gives White excellent attacking chances.

19 ♘f3 ♖e7 20 ♕e1

White prepares to transfer the queen to the kingside.

20...♕f8 21 ♘e5

21...♘xe5?

In a difficult position Black blunders away a piece.

22 fxe5 1-0

It makes sense to activate the queen's bishop before it is locked in behind a wall of pawns. However, White responds actively and thereby persuades Black to go against his original idea.

Pira-Bon

Marseilles 2001

1 d4 d5 2 ♘f3 ♘c6 3 ♗f4 ♗f5

The bishop is developed and in some lines assumes an important role after ...♘b4 putting pressure on c2.

4 e3

4...♘f6

After 4...e6 White can play 5 ♗b5 to pin the knight with play similar to the main game. Alternatively, I think the relatively obscure 5 a3 is worth a try. The odd-looking move is another way of avoiding main lines by delaying c2-c4. That break will come later but by then Black's set-up will be clear, allowing White to focus his initiative. After 5 a3 ♗d6 6 ♗g3 play might continue:

a) 6...h5?! (Black reacts aggressively) 7 c4 h4 8 ♗xd6 ♕xd6 9 ♘c3 dxc4 10 h3 a6 (10...♘a5? is a misguided attempt to hang on to the extra pawn which becomes clear after 11 ♕a4+ ♘c6 12 e4 ♗g6 13 d5 when White is winning) 11 ♗xc4 ♘f6 12 0-0 ♖d8 13 b4 (a useful way to gain space on the queenside and eliminating the resource ...♘a5 when the white queen comes to b3) 13...e5 14 ♕b3! exd4 15 ♖ad1 (the pin allows White to recover the pawn at his leisure) 15...d3 16 ♘a4 ♘e5 17 ♘xe5 ♕xe5 18 ♘c5 (18 ♗xf7+ ♔f8 19 ♘c5 b6 20 ♘xa6 d2 is awkward for White because his pieces lack harmony and there is a passed pawn on the second rank!) 18...0-0 19 ♘xd3 ♗xd3 20 ♖xd3 ♖xd3 21 ♕xd3 (White has a slight edge due to his superior pawn structure and influential bishop) 21...♘e4 22 ♗d5

♘d6 23 ♖c1 c6 24 ♗b3 ♕f6 25 ♖d1 ♖d8 26 e4 g6 27 e5! 1-0 Kacheishvili-Bruch, Gmuend 2001.

b) 6...♘f6 7 c4 0-0 8 ♘c3 ♘e4 9 ♖c1 (White is in no hurry to capture on d5 and prefers to get his pieces activated, while 9 cxd5 exd5 10 ♘xd5? ♗xg3 11 hxg3 ♕xd5 leaves Black a piece up) 9...dxc4 10 ♗xc4 a6 11 ♗d3 ♘xc3 12 ♖xc3 ♗g6 13 0-0 ♖c8 14 ♗xg6 hxg6 15 ♕b3 (a useful move designed to gain time by attacking the b7 pawn) 15...♘a5 16 ♕c2 ♘c6 (Black is never given a chance to advance the c-pawn and is consequently rather passive for the rest of the game) 17 ♕e4 ♗xg3 18 hxg3 ♕d5 19 ♕c2 ♖fd8 20 ♖c5 ♕d6 21 ♖c1 ♕e7 22 ♕e4 ♕f6 23 ♘e5! (with doubled rooks on the c-file White feels it is time to exchange the defending knight on c6) 23...♘xe5 24 dxe5 ♕e7 25 ♕xb7 ♖b8 26 ♕xa6 ♖xb2 27 ♖xc7 ♖d1+ 28 ♔h2 (28 ♖xd1 ♕xc7 29 ♕d6 also wins) 28...♕g5 29 ♖c8+ ♔h7 30 ♖1c4 1-0 Ward-Brameld, St Helier 1999.

5 ♗b5

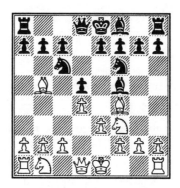

5...♗d7

5...♘d7 was another ploy to block the pin seen in Taimanov-Gonzalez Rabago, Malaga 1999. In that game the former world title contender continued quietly with 6 0-0 and proceeded to exert control after 6...e6 7 c4!? (although the early advance of the c-pawn to c4 is generally avoided in our repertoire there are exceptions. In this case, there is no danger that it will transpose to a main line familiar to Black so it is right to try and undermine the d5 pawn) 7...♗xb1 8 ♖xb1 ♘e7 9 cxd5 exd5 10 b4 (White is wary of allowing any counterplay by a future ...c7-c5) 10...♘g6 11 ♗g3 ♗e7 12 ♕c2 c6 13 ♗d3 0-0 14 b5 (the minority pawn attack works particularly well when it is supported by so many pieces) 14...c5 15 dxc5 ♗xc5 16 ♗f5 (White clears the d-file ready to attack the isolated d-pawn) 16...♖c8 (16...♗e7 does little to save the d-pawn after 17 ♖fd1 ♘f6 18 e4!) 17 ♕d3 ♗b6 18 ♕xd5 with a winning advantage. Taimanov-Gonzalez Rabago, Malaga 1999.

6 0-0

With the bishop on d7 it might be a good idea to consider 6 c4 when play might continue 6...e6 7 0-0 ♘a5 8 ♗xd7+ ♘xd7 9 cxd5 exd5 10 ♘c3 c6 11 e4 offering White the better chances due to his superior development.

6...e6 7 c3

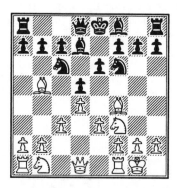

An instructive game because once again White sticks to the usual solid London pawn structure and demonstrates that basic knowledge of the opening strategy is enough to get a decent position.

7...♗d6 8 ♘bd2 0-0 9 ♗d3

Now that Black has submitted to a passive position the light-squared bishop takes up a more prominent attacking role.

9...♘e7 10 ♘e5

Exploiting the fact that in this line White's control of e5 allows his king's knight to occupy that square.

10...♘g6 11 ♗g3 a6

The start of a misguided attempt to engineer some counterplay on the queenside by advancing the pawns. Of course 11...c5? loses to 12 ♘xg6 ♗xg3 13 ♘xf8 when it is time for Black to start counting the material.

12 ♕e2 ♕b8 13 ♘df3

Pira is content to shift his minor pieces towards the kingside in preparation for an attack. One idea might be h2-h4-h5 to disrupt Black's kingside defences.

13...c5?

In an attempt to break free from his restricted position Black goes wrong.

14 ♗xg6 hxg6 15 dxc5 ♗xe5

Unfortunately only now it is clear to Black that 15...♗xc5?? is shattered by 16 ♘xd7.

16 ♘xe5 ♗b5 17 c4 dxc4 18 a4

The first sign of activity by Black is easily dismissed and White remains a pawn up with the much better position.

18...♘e4 19 ♘xg6 ♘xg3 20 ♘e7+

An in-between move, which devastates Black.

20...♔h7 21 fxg3

Watch out! The threat is 22 ♕h5 mate.

21...g6 22 ♕g4 ♕e5

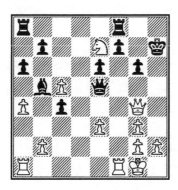

23 ♖xf7+! 1-0

Probably the best continuation is 3...♗g4 to get the bishop into action.

L.Hansen-Fries Nielsen
Danish Championship 1999

1 d4 d5 2 ♘f3 ♘c6 3 ♗f4 ♗g4

I think this is a sensible response because Black is hoping for c2-c4 transposing into normal lines of the Chigorin and ...♗g4 is part of that usual set-up. It is also useful if White responds with a kingside fianchetto because 4 g3 is met by 4...♕d7 when 5 ♗g2 ♗h3 is the sort of position that Chigorin players prefer. Of course, our opening repertoire will not be so obliging for Black.

4 e3 e6 5 ♘bd2

White employs the usual set-up of the London System.

5...♗d6 6 c3!?

This is in keeping with the overall repertoire strategy of maintaining a solid pawn formation by avoiding c2-c4. In the present case, White is not worried about having doubled f-pawns if Black exchanges bishops because that would allow White to exert control over the e5 square which will eventually be occupied by a knight. Also possible is 6 ♗g3.

6...♘ge7

Or 6...♗xf4 7 exf4 ♕d6 8 ♕b3 (this is the standard move although I rather like 8 ♕a4!? because it invites Black to fall for a pretty trap after 8...♗xf3 9 ♘xf3 ♕xf4? and now 10 ♗a6! wins) 8...♗xf3 9 ♘xf3 ♘ge7 10 g3 0-0 11 ♗d3 f6 12 0-0 ♘g6 13 ♖fe1 ♘ce7 14 ♖e2 (intending to double rooks with advantage) 14...♘xf4? 15 gxf4 ♕xf4 16 ♖e3 e5 17 ♖ae1 and White stood clearly better in Kinsman-Martin Ojeda, Chartres 1990.

7 ♗e2 0-0

An attempt to prepare a pawn centre with 7...f6? fails to impress after 8 ♗g3 ♘f5 (8...e5? 9 ♘xe5! ♗xe2 10 ♘xc6 ♗xd1 11 ♘xd8 ♔xd8 12 ♖xd1 leaves White a pawn up in the ending) 9 e4!? ♘xg3 10 hxg3 ♕d7 11 ♕c2. 0-0-0 12 0-0-0 h5?! 13 ♖de1 ♕f7 14 exd5 exd5 15 ♗d3 when the plan of ♘f3-h4-g6 gave White an edge in Fokin-Reprintsev, Russian Cup 1999.

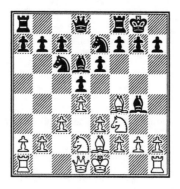

8 h4!?

White announces his intention to attack! The h-pawn is advanced as a way of provoking Black into compromising his kingside pawn structure.

It is also possible to play less adventurously with 8 h3 ♗h5:

a) 9 0-0 (the safe approach) 9...♗xf4 10 exf4 (White has doubled pawns but these help to control the e5 square and give White's rooks access to the semi-open e-file) 10...b6 11 ♖e1 ♘a5 12 ♘f1 ♗xf3 13 ♗xf3 c5 14 ♘e3 c4 15 ♕c2 f5 16 ♖e2, intending to double rooks and target the backward e6 pawn, gave White a plus in Frosch-Schroll, Frohnleiten 2000.

b) 9 g4 ♗g6 10 h4!? (White starts chasing the light-squared bishop to put Black under pressure) 10...f6 11 h5 ♗e8 12 ♗xd6 ♕xd6 13 ♕c2 (having faith in the aggressive kingside pawn advance, White prepares to castle queenside) 13...e5 14 ♘h4 e4 15 ♘g2 ♘d8 16 0-0-0 c5?! (Black wants to galvanise his queenside operations but it merely helps White to activate his queen's knight—16...♗d7!? is a decent alternative offering equal chances) 17 dxc5 ♕xc5 18 ♘f4 ♗f7 19 ♘b3 ♕d6? 20 ♕xe4 with a clear advantage Mira-Hagesaether, Varna 2002

8...f6

A chess maxim proclaims that an attack on the wing should be countered by active play in the centre so Black prepares ...e6-e5.

9 ♗xd6 cxd6 10 h5

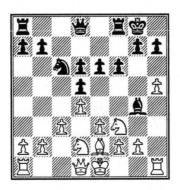

A curious position has arisen where White is threatening to step up the attack with ♘h4 when the exchange of bishops will allow the white queen to enter the fray. Alternatively, simply h5-h6 will be a thorn in the defence.

10...h6?!

10...e5? is the natural response but it comes unstuck after 11 ♘xe5! ♘xe5 12 ♗xg4 ♘d3+ 13 ♔e2 ♘xb2 14 ♗e6+ ♔h8 15 ♕b3 ♘c4 16 ♘xc4 dxc4 17 ♕xb7 winning. Perhaps 10...♕b6!? should be considered with Black trying to deflect White from his kingside attack by counterplay on the other flank.

11 ♘h4! ♗xe2 12 ♕xe2 e5 13 0-0

It may seem surprising that White is not prepared to castle queenside and go for an all-out attack. However the Danish grandmaster is satisfied with having provoked Black into compromising his kingside and now intends to exploit the weakened light squares.

13...f5

Or 13...♕d7 14 ♖ad1 e4 15 f4 f5 16 ♔h2 ♕e6 17 ♖g1 ♕f6 18 ♕f2 intending g2-g4 with a slight edge.

14 f4 ♕d7

If 14...e4 then the tension in the centre is removed allowing White to gradually build-up his forces after 15 ♔h2 by ♖g1 and g2-g4.

15 ♖f2 ♖f6 16 ♖d1

White brings the queen's rook into the action rather than force matters by exchanging pawns.

16...♕e6 17 dxe5 dxe5 18 ♘b3 b6

Once again 18...e4 closes the centre and results in both players manoeuvring behind a wall of pawns which will slightly favour White who has a space advantage. For example: 19 ♔h2 ♖af8 20 ♖g1 ♕f7 21 ♘c5 (21 g4?! fxg4 22 ♖xg4 ♘e5 is better for Black) 21...♘c8 22 ♖ff1 ♔h7 23 ♖d1 with roughly equal chances.

19 ♘f3 ♖e8?! 20 ♕b5 ♖ff8?

The queen's knight is pinned so Black makes an effort to protect the rook on e8. It is typical of such positions that Black has to be very alert to the possible nuances. 20...exf4!? has been suggested as an improvement when play might continue 21 exf4 ♕f7 22 ♖e2! ♕xh5? 23 ♖de1 ♖ff8 (23...♕f7 24 ♘e5 ♘xe5 25 ♖xe5 is in White's favour due to his firm hold on the position with his active pieces) 24 ♘bd4 ♘xd4 25 ♘xd4 ♕f7 26 ♖e5!, intending ♕e2 to add decisive weight to the pin on the e-file, wins.

21 ♘xe5 ♘xe5 22 ♘d4!

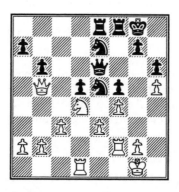

An in-between move which knocks the black queen off its favoured perch. The gain of time is decisive.

22...♘f3+

Fries Nielsen concedes a pawn, which is a long-term worry. Then again, the alternatives are not particularly welcoming: 22...♕f7 23 fxe5 ♕xh5 24 ♖df1 ♔h8 (24...g6 25 ♘e6! wins) 25 ♕d7! when the white queen dominates the board and triggers an avalanche of tactics e.g. 25...g6 26 ♘e6 ♖g8 27 ♖f3 intending ♖f3-h3 is overwhelming or 22...♕f6!? 23 fxe5 ♕xe5 24 ♘xf5! (the key to the sacrifice is that the rook on e8 is also under attack) 24...♘xf5 25 ♖xd5 ♕xe3 26 ♖dxf5 ♖xf5 27 ♕xf5 offers White the superior chances.

23 ♖xf3 ♕c8 24 ♖f2!

A high-class move that makes room for the white knight in order to manoeuvre to an even better square.

24...♔h7 25 ♘f3 ♘g8

What else? It is difficult to find any constructive moves because after 25...♖d8 26 ♖fd2 ♕e6 27 ♘e5 White has a python like grip on the game.

26 ♖xd5 ♖xe3 27 ♖e5

Hansen makes an effort to exchange the only active black piece.

27...♖e4 28 ♘d2 ♖xe5 29 fxe5

White's extra pawn is now passed and Black's pieces are faced with the arduous task of preventing its advance.

29...♕e6 30 a3 ♖d8 31 ♕e2 ♘e7 32 ♘f3 ♖d5 33 ♖f1 ♘c6 34 ♖e1 b5 35 ♕e3! ♕e8

Nor can Black pass by making pawn moves rather than major piece manoeuvres. For example: 35...a6 36 ♕f4 a5 37 ♘d4 ♘xd4 38 cxd4 a4 39 ♖e3 ♔h8 40 ♖c3 with a winning advantage.

36 e6 ♕e7 37 ♕f4 ♔g8 38 ♘d4 ♘xd4 39 cxd4 ♖d6 40 ♕e5 ♖d8 41 b4 1-0

SUMMARY

The game **Grube-Zawierta**, Hagenbach 1998, is a good example of how pedestrian defence is punished by using a standard plan of development. There are no tricky lines for White who just has to continuously improve his pieces. It seems a good idea for Black to develop the queen's bishop at an early stage but **Pira-Bon** shows that aggressive play by White can put Black on the defensive. It is more prudent to play 3...♗g4 as in the heavy-weight encounter **L.Hansen-Fries Nielsen**. One has to admire 8 h4 but for those of a nervous disposition I have included an alternative!

THE DUTCH

Popular with club players the Dutch Defence is an attempt by Black to seize the initiative with 1...f5. It is also popular at international level and has been employed by world champions such as Alekhine and Botvinnik. Basically it can be divided into two categories—one with and one without a kingside fianchetto for Black. As usual I have tried to find easy-to-learn and clear-cut plans, whilst not forgetting to point out various traps and pitfalls.

HISTORY OF THE LENINGRAD DUTCH

The Leningrad Dutch is so-called in honour of the group of Leningrad masters, including Kopylov, Korchnoi, Kuzminikh and Vinogradov, who in the 1940s developed a new brand of Dutch which was to rapidly attract the attention of the chess world. Possibly influenced by the growing popularity of the King's Indian Defence, the Leningraders experimented with a kingside fianchetto in the Dutch, whereas previously the king's bishop had been developed on e7 or d6. Nowadays the opening is more popular than ever with novelties and nuances constantly being added to the theory of both main and side-lines.

IDEAS BEHIND THE OPENING

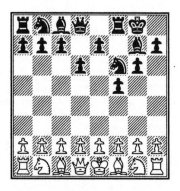

This is the set-up that Black is aiming for after the first six moves. If possible Black would like to play ...e7-e5 so that the two pawns on the fifth rank will exert some influence on the centre. Another plan is to transfer his queen via e8-h5 to launch an attack on the castled king which can be increased by ...h7-h6 and ...g6-g5 and sometimes an even further advance of the kingside pawns. However it is White who usually dictates matters, leaving Black merely responding defensively to the pressure that is being applied in the early stages.

HOW TO BEAT THE LENINGRAD DUTCH

I have tried to find a way to incorporate some of the themes from the Barry Attack but there are no new developments in lines with ♗f4. This is why I recommend instead a line which avoids any nasty traps and forces Black to enter a position that is relatively unknown.

1 d4 f5 2 g3 ♘f6 3 ♗g2 g6 4 ♘f3 ♗g7 5 0-0 0-0 6 b4

This is a great idea to gain space on the queenside and at the same time shock your opponent. It looks a bit weird but it has been tested by some of the world's top players and the results are positive. White declares his intention to advance on the queenside and he will also keep an eye on the centre by retaining the option of e2-e4 at an appropriate moment. The old solid but slow idea was to play c2-c4 followed by b2-b3, a2-a3 and b3-b4. Quite a contrast to the text which is more dynamic and aggressive and attempts to assert White's superiority straight out of the opening. It is also worth noting that many lines featuring ...♘c6, in order to help support the advance ...e7-e5, now fail to convince since White can simply play b4-b5 kicking the knight away.

As usual in the Dutch, Black's play is based on monitoring the centre and creating a kingside attack. However, the swift advance of the queenside pawns tends to distract Black's pieces from their normal duties because they now have to cope with a fresh set of problems.

Van Wely-Guliev
European Championship, Ohrid 2001

1 d4 f5

Black stakes a claim in the centre by striving to control the e4 square.

2 g3 ♘f6 3 ♗g2

I think this is the best way to develop the light-squared bishop. The influence on the h1-a8 diagonal is important because it helps to control the vital central e4 and d5 squares, while the pressure on the b7 pawn will sometimes be significant when the c8 bishop moves.

3...g6 4 ♘f3 ♗g7

The bishop on g7 is well placed to exert pressure on the central d4 pawn.

5 0-0 d6

Black is getting on with the job of developing his pieces.

6 b4!?

A sign that White wishes to expand on the queenside with his pawns and gain a space advantage.

6...0-0

Guliev responds with the standard move in this set-up. In the long-term Black would like to play ...e7-e5 when the two pawns in the centre will give him good chances. Of course, with a white pawn already on b4, the option of ...♘c6—to promote ...e7-e5—is neutralised because then the simple b4-b5 will kick the knight away. The other possiblilities of 6...a5 and 6...d5 are discussed later in the chapter.

7 ♗b2

Development aimed at restraining ...e7-e5.

7...♕e8

The queen shifts to the kingside to promote a timely and appropriate ...e7-e5 and create the possibility of ...♕e8-h5 to help initiate an attack. In the game Anand-De la Riva Aguado, Villarrobledo 2001, Black tried 7...c6 to contain White's pawn rush on the queenside. There followed 8 c4 ♔h8 9 ♘bd2 ♗e6 (the reason why the black king moved to the corner is revealed—10 ♘g5 can now be met by 10...♗g8) 10 ♕c2 ♘bd7 11 a4 ♗g8 12 a5 with a space advantage on the queenside.

8 c4 h6

If Black is very keen to follow the standard plan of forcing through 8...e7-e5 he might consider 8...♘g4, which occurred in Lautier-Reinderman, Mondariz zonal 2000. That game went 9 ♘c3 (now that the black knight has moved White spots the chance for his own knight to occupy the d5 square without fear of being exchanged) 9...e5 10 ♘d5 ♖f7 11 h3 ♘h6 12 dxe5 dxe5 13 ♘g5 (it is worth noting that it is White's lead in development that enables him to create tactical chances) 13...♖d7 14 ♕a4 c6? 15 ♘b6! axb6 16 ♕xa8 and White had a winning advantage.

9 ♘bd2

This is a good square for the knight because the obvious move 9 ♘c3?! runs into 9...♕f7, threatening the pawn at c4, an idea employed by the English player Stuart Conquest. A sample line is 10 ♕b3 c6 11 ♖ad1 ♘bd7 12 b5 ♘b6 and it is Black who has the initiative.

9...g5

Black decides to advance his g-pawn because the usual plan of ...e7-e5 is not possible because that square is well covered by White's pieces.

10 e3 f4?!

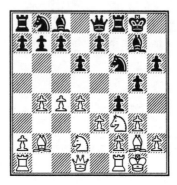

Black does not want to just wait and be overrun on the queenside so he pushes forward at once on the other flank. The only snag is that such aggressive play needs to be backed up by active piece play which can hardly be properly implemented when the queenside pieces remain on their starting squares! 10...g4 has been suggested as a possible alternative but the key factor is Black's poor development which leaves him wide open to tactical traps. For instance: 11 ♘h4 e5 (at last Black manages to advance the e-pawn but 10...e6 should be treated with respect by 12 ♕c2 when 12...♘bd7 13 d5! is fine for White) 12 dxe5 dxe5 13 e4 f4 14 gxf4 exf4 15 e5 ♘fd7 16 ♕xg4 ♘xe5 17 ♗d5+ ♔h8 18 ♕g2 when White has the superior chances due to his active piece play. The immediate threat is ♗xe5 followed by ♘g6+ winning material.

11 exf4 gxf4 12 ♖e1!

The rook moves to the e-file to target the e7 pawn and ensure the black queen has to take on a defensive role. Instead 12 gxf4? wins a pawn but plunges White into difficulties upon 12...♘h5!, intending ...♘xf4 and ...♕g6 with attacking chances.

12...fxg3 13 hxg3 ♗g4 14 ♕c2

Van Wely moves the queen out of the way of the pin and targets the weakened g6 square.

14...♘c6 15 b5 ♘d8 16 ♘h4 ♕d7 17 ♘f1!

A grandmaster move! The knight aims to take advantage of the weak light squares in Black's camp by the manoeuvre ♘f1-e3 intending a future ♘f5.

17...♖f7 18 ♘e3 ♗h3 19 ♕g6 ♗xg2 20 ♔xg2 e6

The pawn move is designed to stop a knight coming to f5.

21 d5!

There is no stopping White from gaining the f5 square and also adding the queen's bishop to the escalating attack.

21...♘h7

If 21...♔h8 White gets the chance to win in style by 22 ♘ef5! exf5 23 ♘xf5 (the big threat is 24 ♘xg7 ♖xg7 25 ♗xf6 winning) 23...♘h5 24 ♘xg7 ♘xg7 25 ♕xh6+ ♔g8 26 ♖h1 threatening ♕h8+ and Black is busted.

22 ♘g4 ♔f8

Black just drops a piece for nothing. However, perhaps it was just a desperate ploy to avoid having his name linked to a famous loss and end up appearing again and again in chess puzzle books. Why? Well after the obvious 22...♔h8 Van Wely could have unleashed the star move 23 ♕xg7+!! when Black is mated after 23...♖xg7 24 ♘g6+ ♔g8 25 ♘xh6.

23 ♕xh7 ♗xb2 24 ♘g6+ 1-0

Naturally, when faced with an unusual choice of opening there will be a desire to try and punish White's outlandish b-pawn advance. However in reality there is no such refutation although 6...a5 is likely to be a spirited try...

Schandorff-Glienke
Roskilde 1998

1 d4 f5 2 g3 ♘f6 3 ♗g2 g6 4 ♘f3 ♗g7 5 0-0 0-0 6 b4 a5!?
Black loses no time in challenging White's supremacy on the queenside.

7 b5

The pawn ventures forward and has already stopped Black from playing ...♘c6. Of course, 7 bxa5 is exactly what Black wants because after 7...♖xa5 the rook is activated with long-term threats against the a2-pawn.

7...d6

The main alternative 7...d5, to secure the c4 and e4 squares, is worth a close look. The best response is to play aggressively with 8 c4! when Leitao-Santos, Sao Paulo 2000, continued 8...dxc4 9 ♕a4 c6 (9...♗e6 10 ♘g5! {the bishop cannot retreat safely and Black is obliged to enter the complications} 10...♗d5 11 ♗xd5+ ♕xd5 12 ♘c3 ♕xd4 13 ♘f3! ♕xc3 {13...♕c5 14 ♗a3 is good for White} 14 ♗d2 ♕b2 15 ♖ab1 traps the black queen making White the favourite to win) 10 ♕xc4+ ♕d5 11 ♕xd5+ ♘xd5 (11...cxd5 seems obvious but White can develop smoothly after 12 ♗a3 ♖e8 13 ♘c3 e6 14 ♘a4 ♘bd7 15 ♖ac1 when White is threatening to move a rook to the seventh) 12 a4 ♘b4 (12...c5 is possible when 13 ♗b2 maintains White's advantage in development) 13 ♘a3! ♘d7 14 ♘c4 ♘c5?! (14...♘c2 is important because it seems that Black can win the d-pawn but 15 ♖b1 is good for White after 15...cxb5 {15...♘xd4 16 ♘xd4 ♗xd4 17 bxc6 bxc6 18 ♗xc6} 16 ♖xb5 ♗xd4 17 ♗h6 ♗g7 {17...♖e8 runs into 18 ♖c1 and White wins a piece} 18 ♗xg7 ♔xg7 19 ♖c1 ♘b4 20 ♘xa5) 15 ♗g5! (now the rooks are connected there are mounting threats such as ♗xe7 and dxc5—however the immediate 15 dxc5 allows Black to survive after 15...♗xa1) 15...cxb5 16 ♘b6 ♘xa4 17 ♘xa8 with a winning advantage.

8 ♗b2

The queenside fianchetto helps to stop the advance ...e7-e5.

8...c6 9 a4 ♘e4 10 ♘bd2

The knight on e4 is Black's most active piece so White wants to exchange it and in the process maintain his lead in development.

10...♘xd2 11 ♕xd2 ♗e6?!

It is understandable that Glienke is eager to get the rest of his pieces into the game but the more cautious 11...♔h8!? is necessary so that after 12...♗e6 he can meet 13 ♘g5 with 13...♗g8.

12 ♘g5 ♗d7

I suspect that 12...♗d5? was the original intention but after 13 ♗xd5+ cxd5 14 ♘e6 the knight forks the queen and rook.

13 ♕e3 d5

If 13...♖e8 then 14 ♘e6 ♗xe6 15 ♕xe6+ ♔h8 16 c4 secures White an edge because Black cannot easily develop his queenside since the knight is tied to the defence of the pawn on c6.

14 c4!

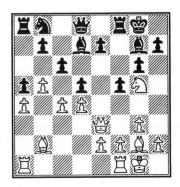

White could try to defend the b5 pawn but rightly rejects a quiet line in favour of something more aggressive. It is worth noting that c4 is often played against ...d5 to ensure that Black does not consolidate the pawns in the centre. Another example of White's approach can be found in the note to Black's seventh move. As usual in the Dutch the root of Black's problems lies in his failure to activate the queenside forces.

14...dxc4 15 ♘e6 ♗xe6 16 ♕xe6+ ♔h8 17 ♕xc4 ♖a7

A novel way of protecting the b-pawn, which is understandable in view of the fact that the rook is not doing much on a8 and the knight is riveted to its starting square to protect the c6 pawn. However it cannot be good to place a rook on a square where it is so severely restricted and ineffective. To add to Black's problems 17...cxb5 18 ♕xb5 allows White strong pressure against b7 and 18...♗xd4? is ruled out by 19 ♖ad1 e5 20 e3 winning.

18 ♖fd1 cxb5 19 ♕xb5 ♖f6 20 ♗a3

A good example of the power of the bishop pair which can cover so many important squares and thus create plenty of tactical opportunities. The immediate threat here is 20 ♗c5.

20...♘c6

If 20...♖b6 then 21 ♗xe7! is excellent for White, e.g. 21...♖xb5 (21...♕c7? allows 22 ♕e8+ ♗f8 23 ♕xf8 mate or 21...♕xe7 22 ♕xb6 with a winning advantage) 22 ♗xd8 ♖b2 23 ♖ac1 intending ♖c1-c8.

21 ♗c5 ♖a8 22 ♖ab1

If you see a good move then look for a better one! Schandorff could have taken the pawn with 22 ♕xb7 but Black is given a glimmer of hope after 22...♖b8 23 ♕a6 ♘b4 24 ♕c4 f4, although it has to be said that White is still better.

22...♖b8 23 ♗xc6 ♖xc6 24 d5 ♖f6

An indication of White's superiority is revealed by the fact that 24...♖cc8 allows White to go on the rampage with 25 d6! when play might continue 25...exd6 26 ♗xd6 ♖a8 27 ♗e5 (the discovered attack on the queen quickly decides the game) 27...♕e7 28 ♗xg7+ ♕xg7 29 ♖d7 ♕f6 30 ♕xb7 with victory in sight.

25 ♗b6 ♕f8 26 ♗c7 ♖a8 27 ♕xb7

Finally White has found time to pick up an extra pawn while Black remains in a defensive state and with no sign of counterplay.

27...♖fa6 28 ♖dc1 ♗f6 29 ♗b8!

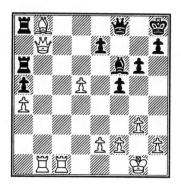

1-0

Black resigned in view of the threat ♖c1-c8 while 29...♔g7 is well met by 30 ♖c6 ♖xc6 31 dxc6 winning.

There is another way for Black to respond to White's unusual set-up and that is with 6...d5 to fight for control of the c4 and e4 squares.

Mikhalchishin-Kavcić
Slovenian Championship 1997

1 d4 f5 2 g3 ♘f6 3 ♗g2 g6 4 ♘f3 ♗g7 5 0-0 0-0 6 b4 d5

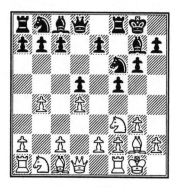

This move has not been played much because Leningrad players are used to striving for the standard plan of ...d7-d6 and ...e7-e5 and the text takes them to unknown territory. This is of course encouraging for White but nevertheless the move does have the merit of fighting for control of the c4 and e4 squares.

7 ♗b2

Mikhalchishin is not concerned by Black's relatively unusual set-up and continues with the normal plan of a queenside development that helps to control the e5 square—which is likely to be occupied by a white knight. On the other hand, if Black plants a knight on e4 then this can always be dislodged by a timely f2-f3.

7...c6 8 ♘bd2 ♗e6?!

A typical mistake by Black whose priority is to develop his dormant queenside. However the text needs to be prepared with ...♔h8 so that after ...♗e6 there is the possibility of retreating the bishop to g8 after ♘g5.

9 ♘g5 ♗f7 10 c4

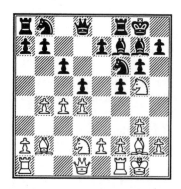

It is important for White to challenge the pawn on d5 otherwise Black will be able to develop easily by ...♘bd7-b6 and reinforce his control of the c4 square.

10...♘a6

Or 10...dxc4 11 ♘xf7 ♖xf7 12 ♘xc4 with a slight advantage.

11 b5 ♘c7 12 bxc6 bxc6 13 ♘xf7 ♖xf7 14 ♕a4

On a4 the queen exerts pressure against c6 and allows the rooks to co-ordinate.

14...♘e4 15 ♘b3 ♖b8

15...♕e8 is a safe bet although after 16 ♖fc1, threatening 17 cxd5, White's extra manoeuvring space assures him the advantage.

16 ♖fc1

Simple chess is often the best way forward. 16 ♕xa7? is not possible because of 16...dxc4, winning a piece, so White defends the c4 pawn thereby renewing the threat against a7. At first glance 16 ♕xc6 looks tempting but 16...♖f6 is a killer move because after 17 ♕a4 Black wins by 17...♖a6 as the white queen has run out of escape squares.

16...♞d6 17 cxd5 cxd5 18 ♖xc7!

A tactical breakthrough that nets White a pawn and an even better position.

18...♛xc7 19 ♗xd5 ♛c2 20 ♛xa7 ♖xb3 21 ♗xb3 ♛xb2

At first glance it seems that, despite all his endeavours, White will only get two pieces for a rook. But he has seen a little further than his opponent...

22 ♛b8+! 1-0

Black did not wait for 22...♗f8 23 ♗xf7+ ♞xf7 24 ♛xb2.

CLASSICAL STONEWALL

HISTORY OF THE OPENING

The Stonewall rose to prominence in the 19th century when players would use the solid pawn formation to keep White at bay in the centre long enough to create a kingside attack. Since defensive techniques have somewhat improved since those days, there is now an acknowledgement by strong players that Black has to take more care of his queenside and the centre.

IDEAS BEHIND THE OPENING

The Stonewall Dutch can be recognised by Black's pawn formation of f5-e6-d5-c6. Practice has shown that with the centre fairly fixed Black tends to try and create attacking chances on the kingside by ...♛d8-e8-h5 and through an advance of the kingside pawns initiated by ...h7-h6 and ...g7-g5.

HOW TO BEAT THE CLASSICAL STONEWALL

The drawback of Black's pawn formation is that the light-squared bishop is blocked in behind the wall of pawns which makes it difficult to activate the queenside. Also it means that the dark squares are sensitive and Black usually has to be careful to hang on to his king's bishop or know how to play actively. There are a number of tried and trusted responses for White but I would like to explore a side-line which Black will not be expecting. In common with the lines arising from the Barry Attack the key to this variation is the development of the queen's bishop to f4 to try and take advantage of the weak dark squares in Black's position.

Macieja-Lesiège
Bermuda 2001

1 d4 f5 2 g3 ♘f6 3 ♗g2 e6 4 ♘f3 d5 5 ♗f4

The queen's bishop is developed to reinforce White's control over the important e5 square

5...♗e7

Black carries on with kingside development and avoids the exchange of bishops with ...♗d6, which is discussed in the next game.

6 c4

Once Black indicates a desire to create a stonewall pawn formation with pawns on d5, e6 and f5 then White should advance the c-pawn in order to fight for control of the centre.

6...c6

6...dxc4 releases the tension in the centre in favour of White who can win back the pawn with 7 ♘e5 or even 7 ♕a4+.

7 0-0 0-0 8 ♘bd2

White brings the knight to d2 so that in the long-term he can try to open the c-file. The usual move used to be 8 ♘c3 but that makes the game plan more awkward because time is wasted moving the knight out of the way to clear the c-file.

8...b6

Also possible is 8...♘e4 which is a standard idea in the opening and takes advantage of the fact that the d and f-pawns support the knight. White can respond with the plan that I am recommending in the main game—namely to make use of the c-file with 9 ♖c1. For instance: 9...g5 10 ♗xb8 ♘xd2 11 ♕xd2 ♖xb8 12 b4 (if in doubt White can always rely on the plan of advancing the queenside pawns) 12...♗d7 13 ♘e5 ♗f6 (13...♗d6? keeps an eye on the b-pawn but runs into 14 ♘xd7 ♕xd7 15 ♕xg5+ winning) 14 ♕e3 (White does not want Black to capture on e5 and be obliged to take back with the d-pawn because the resulting doubled pawn would be awkward to defend and a liability) 14...♗e8 15 b5 (this consistent push of the b-pawn enables White to expertly undermine the d5 pawn) 15...cxb5 16 cxd5 exd5 17 ♖c5 when the d-pawn will soon be captured, leaving White with the advantage, Romanishin-Sielaff, Dresden 1998.

9 ♕c2 ♗b7 10 ♖ac1

This is what Macieja was planning when he moved his queen's knight to d2. The point is that White can easily develop while Black has to be wary of his weaknesses, e.g. a natural move such as 10...♘bd7? would allow 11 ♘g5! when the e6 pawn cannot be defended.

10...♘e4 11 ♘e5 ♘d7 12 cxd5

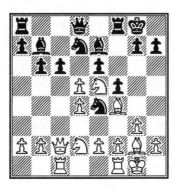

12...♘xe5?!

An obvious reply because ideally Black would like to take back on d5 with the e-pawn to keep the queen out of c7. Of course, 12...exd5 13 ♘xc6 just loses a pawn while the best try 12...cxd5 13 ♕c7! (the whole point of doubling on the c-file is to try and infiltrate the seventh rank) 13...♘xe5 14 ♕xe5 ♗c8 15 ♘xe4 dxe4 16 ♖fd1, intending d4-d5, gives White an edge.

13 d6!

There is no point allowing Black to support the centre by taking back on d5 with a pawn. Instead 13 ♗xe5 exd5 offers equal chances.

13...♘xd6

13...♗xd6 does not distract White from gaining an initiative after 14 ♘xe4 ♘f7 (or 14...♘f3+ 15 ♗xf3 ♗xf4 16 gxf4 fxe4 17 ♕xe4 and Black is just a pawn down for nothing) 15 ♘xd6 ♘xd6 16 ♖fd1 when White's powerful bishop pair gives him the advantage.

14 dxe5 ♘b5 15 ♘b3

There is no hurry to take the c-pawn. In fact 15 ♗xc6? is greedy and cleverly punished by 15...♖c8 16 ♕b3 ♖xc6 17 ♕xb5 ♖xc1 18 ♖xc1 g5 19 ♗e3 f4 and after the series of exchanges the bishop has run out of decent squares.

15...g5

Defending the c6 pawn with 15...♖c8 would allow White to exploit his space advantage to mobilise his forces decisively. A sample line: 16 ♖fd1 ♕e8 17 ♕c4! (a nice way to deflect the black queen from its defence of the d7 square) 17...♕f7 (17...♘c7 allows 18 ♗xc6 and White is a pawn up) 18 ♖d7 ♖c7 19 ♖cd1 ♖fc8 20 a4 ♖xd7 21 ♖xd7 ♘c7 22 ♗g5 when the pin along the seventh rank ensures victory.

16 a4 ♖c8

A sign of a good player is the way he continues to hang on and make life hard for an attacker. In this case Black finds an interesting way to try and complicate matters. 16...♘a3!?, to double the a-pawns, is worth a try although 17 bxa3 gxf4 18 ♕c4! is good for White. Alternatively 16...♘c7 is not much use either because 17 ♗xc6 ♗xc6 18 ♕xc6 gxf4 19 ♖fd1 ♕c8 (19...♘d5 20 ♕xe6+ wins) 20 ♕xc7 leaves White clearly on top.

17 ♖fd1 ♕e8 18 ♗d2

It is worth noting how White correctly keeps the pieces on the board because this makes life harder for Black who has cramped pieces and little room to manoeuvre. Also good but less decisive is 18 axb5 cxb5 19 ♕d2 ♖xc1 20 ♖xc1 ♗xg2 21 ♗xg5 ♗d5 22 ♘d4 with the better chances.

18...♘c7 19 ♗xc6 ♗xc6 20 ♕xc6

The first half of the game is complete because White has managed to convert his space advantage into material gain. However to clinch the win it is necessary to know what to do next and how to use the extra pawn and greater mobility to best effect. The rest is a model example of how to make Black suffer.

20...♔f7 21 ♘d4 h6

Or 21...♕xc6 22 ♘xc6 and if 22...a6? (otherwise Black will just lose another pawn) then 23 ♘a7 wins at least the exchange.

22 ♕b7 ♘d5

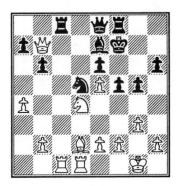

If White grabs a pawn with 22...♕xa4 then the quiet move 23 ♗e1!, defending the knight, leaves Black's position in ruins: 23...♖fd8 (23...♘a6 24 ♖xc8 ♖xc8 25 b3 wins) 24 b3 ♕d7 25 ♘xf5 ♕xd1 26 ♖xd1 ♖xd1 27 ♘d6+ and Black can give up.

23 ♘xf5!

A wonderful move that breaks down Black's pawn barrier thanks to a tactical trick.

23...♖xc1

If the knight is taken with 23...exf5 then 24 ♕xd5+ ♔g7 25 ♕b7 leaves White a couple of pawns up with a tremendous position.

24 ♗xc1 ♔g6 25 ♖xd5!

Another sacrifice to break down any resistance.

25...♖xf5

White is presented with an assortment of strong attacking plans after 25...exd5 with the simplest line ending in a mating net after 26 ♘xe7+ ♔h5 27 f3 g4 (27...♖f7 28 g4+ ♔h4 29 ♔g2 ♖xe7 30 ♗d2!, intending ♗e1 mate, is a pretty way to finish the game) 28 ♔g2 gxf3+ 29 ♔h3!, threatening 30 g4, signals the end for Black.

26 ♖d7 ♗c5 27 ♖g7+ ♔h5 28 g4+

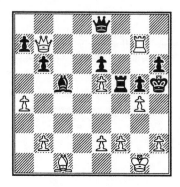

1-0

Black resigned rather than be checkmated after 28...♔xg4 29 ♕g2+ ♔h4 30 ♕g3+ ♔h5 31 ♕h3.

Another approach for Black is to develop the king's bishop on d6. In the following example White comes up with an independent plan to put Black under pressure straight from the opening.

Romanishin-Spinelli

Torino 2000

1 d4 f5 2 g3 ♘f6 3 ♗g2 e6 4 ♘f3 d5 5 ♗f4 ♗d6 6 ♗e5!?

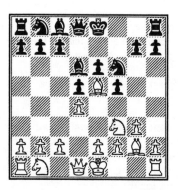

A speciality of the strong grandmaster Romanishin who has added a modern twist to this line—which readers can adopt with confidence. White is reluctant to play 6 ♗xd6 as then 6...cxd6 will cover the important e5 square, whereas an exchange of bishops on e5 will enable White to recapture with the d-pawn and then proceed to undermine the centre by c2-c4. If White chooses to follow the old plan of 6 e3 then Black is presented with a variety of set-ups such as taking on f4 to double the f-pawns or even ...0-0, ...♘e4 and ...g5.

6...c6

It is at this stage of the game that Black is likely to play something different so I have made an effort to explore likely alternatives:

a) 6...0-0 7 0-0 ♗d7 (7...b5!? {this looks odd but the idea is to prevent c2-c4} 8 c3 ♗b7 9 ♘bd2 ♘e4 10 a4 gave White the initiative in Romanishin-Vaisser, Biel 1995) 8 c4 dxc4 9 ♘bd2 ♗c6 (9...b5 only temporarily hangs on to the extra pawn: 10 ♗xf6 gxf6 {10...♕xf6 11 ♘e5 c6 12 ♘xd7 ♘xd7 13 ♗xc6 is good for White} 11 a4 c6 12 ♘h4 ♕b6 13 axb5 ♕xb5 14 ♕c2 wins back a pawn and Black's pawn formation has been severely weakened) 10 ♘xc4 ♗xe5 11 dxe5 ♘g4 (11...♕xd1 12 ♖fxd1 ♘g4 13 h3 ♘h6 14 ♖ac1 when the harmony of White's pieces gives him the advantage.) 12 ♕b3 ♘a6 13 h3 ♘h6 14 ♖fd1 with roughly equal chances, Romanishin-Tu Hoang Thong, Moscow 1994.

b) 6...♘c6 7 c4 dxc4 8 ♘bd2 0-0 (if Black tries to retain the extra pawn by 8...b5 then White can undermine this support by 9 a4 when play might continue 9...♗b7! 10 axb5 ♘xe5 11 dxe5 ♗xe5 12 ♘xc4 ♗d6 13 0-0 with equal chances) 9 0-0 ♗xe5 10 dxe5 ♘d7 11 ♘xc4 ♕e7 12 ♖c1 (it could be argued that the chances are even but it is easier for White to bring his pieces into the action) 12...♖b8 13 ♕d2 ♖d8 14 ♕c3 ♘b6 (in a cramped position it is a good idea to exchange pieces) 15 ♘xb6 axb6 16 ♖fd1 ♖xd1+ 17 ♖xd1 ♗d7 18 ♘d4 ♘xd4 19 ♖xd4 when White's greater mobility of pieces gave him the advantage and he eventually won, Romanishin-Knaak, Dresden 1988.

7 0-0 0-0 8 ♘bd2

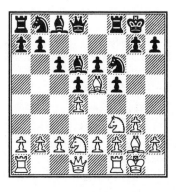

The knight is developed to d2 in order to keep the c-file open for White's queen's rook. This is an echo of the previous illustrative game, Macieja-Lesiège.

8...b6

Black wants to fianchetto on the queenside in order to try and activate his light-squared bishop, which usually remains passive behind the line of pawns on c6-d5-e6-f5.

9 c4 ♕e7 10 ♖c1

In keeping with the plan of exerting pressure on the c-file, White swings the rook across to the c-file.

10...♗b7 11 c5 bxc5?!

Perhaps Black should consider 11...♗xe5 12 ♘xe5 when White has just a small edge.

12 ♗xd6 ♕xd6 13 ♕b3! ♕e7 14 ♖xc5

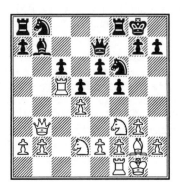

It now becomes clear that Black has a long-term problem with the backward c-pawn.

14...♘a6

Black finally mobilises the queen's knight but it is awkwardly placed on the edge of the board where it has little room to manoeuvre. It just goes to show why 13 ♕b3 was good because it stopped the possibility of 14...♘bd7? on which now follows 15 ♕xb7.

15 ♖a5 ♕c7 16 ♕a3 ♕b6

After 16...♘b8 White hardly wants to fall for 17 ♖xa7 ♖xa7 18 ♕xa7 ♘a6 intending ...♖a8 trapping his queen—but the improvement 17 ♘b3 ♘bd7 18 ♖c1, with the idea of ♘c5, gives White the advantage.

17 ♘b3 ♘e4 18 ♘e5 ♗c8

Black can also deal with the threat of a fork on d7 by 18...♖fd8 when 19 ♕e7, hitting the e6 pawn, is a winner after 19...♘c7 20 ♘d7 ♖xd7 21 ♕xd7.

19 ♖c1

Now that Black's bishop is confined to defence of the d7 square it makes sense to create a direct attack against the c6 pawn, the defence of which it has now relinquished. A clear case of how to grind Black down by continuously improving White's position.

19...♘b4 20 ♘c5

The knight on c5 renews the threat of a fork on d7, at the same time presenting the knight on b4 with the problem of retreating to a safe square.

20...♘d6 21 e3

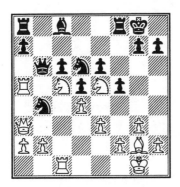

A classy move. White notices that he can rule out any counterplay associated with the queen taking the d-pawn and still win comfortably. Then again there is nothing wrong with 21 ♘ed7, forking the queen and rook, when 21...♗xd7 22 ♘xd7 ♕xd4 23 ♘xf8 ♔xf8 24 ♕c3 looks very good to me.

21...♖d8 22 ♗f1

The motive behind the previous move. Now it becomes obvious that the knight on b4 has nowhere to hide.

22...♘f7 23 ♘xf7 ♔xf7 24 ♖c3 ♗d7 25 ♖b3 ♘c2

25...♖ab8 does not really help because of 26 ♖xa7 ♔e8 27 ♖a4 when the pinned knight will be lost.

26 ♖xb6 ♘xa3 27 ♖b7 1-0

ILYIN-ZHENEVSKY SYSTEM

HISTORY OF THE OPENING

This opening is named after the Soviet master who played it extensively in the 1920s and 30s. It is still popular today and for completeness I have added it to the survey on the Dutch.

IDEAS BEHIND THE OPENING

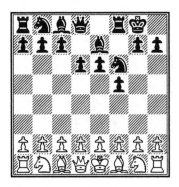

If White plays casually then Black will react with ...♕e8, ...♗d8 and ...e6-e5 to gain influence in the centre and a possible kingside attack by ...♕e8-h5.

HOW TO BEAT THE ILYIN-ZHENEVSKY SYSTEM

I think White should stick to play similar to what has been proposed in other variations and go for a rapid pawn expansion on the queenside with an early b2-b4. This will have the effect of instantly putting Black under pressure and distracting him from his plan of ...e6-e5. Also, if Black embarks upon a premature kingside attack then the recommended response is to try and open the centre to take advantage of Black's neglected queenside development.

The next game is a good example of how to deal with a typical decision by Black to go for an all-out attack on the kingside, regardless of whatever is happening on the rest of the board.

Biriukov-Vager
St Petersburg 1997

1 d4 f5 2 g3 d6 3 ♗g2 ♘f6 4 ♘f3 e6 5 c4 ♗e7 6 0-0 0-0 7 b4!?

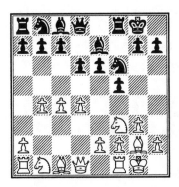

White declares his intention to start a pawn storm on the queenside. One idea is that a queenside fianchetto will help to prevent ...e6-e5 but, with a pawn on b4 rather than b3, it also means that some lines featuring ...♘b8-c6 are not so effective as there is the possibility of b4-b5.

7...♛e8

The queen on e8 is an essential part of the system because it helps support ...e6-e5 after ...♗e7-d8 and might also leap to h5 to contribute to a kingside attack. We are now at a crossroads where Black has various choices:

a) 7...♘e4 8 ♗b2 a5 9 a3 (a matter of taste because 9 b5 is also reasonable) 9...axb4 10 axb4 ♖xa1 11 ♗xa1 b5?! (Black is not willing to sit back and defend so he goes on the offensive—the idea is that by giving up a pawn he can obtain an outpost for his knight on d5 as compensation) 12 cxb5 ♘d7 13 d5! when White has occupied the important d5 square, ensuring an advantage, Krush-Pert, Hastings 2001/2.

b) 7...a5 8 b5 (of course 8 a3? is not possible as 8...axb4 wins a pawn due to the pin on the a-pawn) 8...♛e8 9 ♗b2 ♘bd7 10 ♘bd2 ♛h5 11 ♛c2 g5 12 e4! (the right way to counter a quick kingside attack is to open the centre in order to activate the white pieces) 12...g4 13 ♘e1 e5 14 exf5 exd4 15 ♘b3 ♘c5 16 ♘xd4 when the extra pawn gave White an advantage in Umanskaya-Struchkova, St Petersburg 1996.

c) 7...e5 8 dxe5 dxe5 9 ♘xe5 ♛xd1 (after 9...♗xb4 10 ♛b3!, threatening c4-c5+ followed by ♘f7+, gives White the better chances) 10 ♖xd1 ♗xb4 11 ♘d3 ♗e7 12 ♗f4 with a slight edge in the ending, Levitt-S.Williams, British Team Championship 2000.

8 ♗b2 ♛h5?!

Signalling his intention to go for a direct attack. However it might be better for Black to develop the queenside by 8...♘bd7 and after 9 ♘bd2 to solidify the centre by 9...♘e4 (9...♕h5 10 ♕c2 transposes to the main game) 10 ♘xe4 fxe4 11 ♘d2 d5 12 ♕b3 c6 13 b5 with roughly equal chances, Baburin-Heidenfeld, Kilkenny 2000.

9 ♘bd2 ♘bd7 10 ♕c2

As a reaction to Black's 'blitz' attack on the kingside, White prepares e2-e4 opening the centre and activating his forces.

10...e5!? 11 dxe5 dxe5 12 c5!

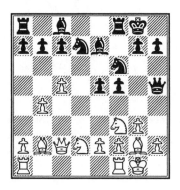

A clear case of the value of having a pawn already on b4 which can support this important advance opening up the a2-g8 diagonal for the white queen. Less enticing are 12 ♗xe5 ♘xe5 13 ♘xe5 ♗xb4 and 12 ♘xe5 ♘xe5 13 ♗xe5 ♗xb4 which both lead to equality.

12...e4 13 ♘d4 ♘e5 14 f4!

It might seem surprising that Biriukov is encouraging Black to put a knight on g4 but this is all part of his plan to repel the attack.

14...♘eg4 15 ♕b3+ ♔h8 16 h3 ♘h6

The attack has been successfully beaten back and White is now on top. It seems that 16...♗d7 is perhaps worth a try since 17 hxg4 leads to complications. For instance: 17...♘xg4 18 ♖fd1 ♕h2+ 19 ♔f1 e3! 20 ♘2f3 ♕xg3 21 ♔g1 ♕f2+ 22 ♔h1 ♖f6 actually wins. However, the cautious 17 ♖fd1 immediately solves the problem because then White is threatening to take on g4 and then cover the vital h2 square by ♘f1.

17 ♖fd1 c6 18 ♘c4

The knight is heading for one of the vacant squares on d6 or e5. White has a strong position because he can gradually increase the scope of his pieces by the simple plan of doubling the rooks on the d-file. This is in marked contrast to Black who has already had his attack repulsed and must now adopt a wait and see policy.

18...♘f7 19 ♖d2 ♘d5

A temporary measure to block the d-file so as to give Black time to start mobilising his queenside.

20 ♖ad1 ♕g6 21 ♔h2 ♗d7 22 ♘e3

White sensibly seeks to exchange Black's useful knight and at the same time open the d-file for future use by the white rooks.

22...♘xe3 23 ♕xe3 ♗e6 24 g4!

An excellent way to break up the pawn chain—weakening it at its base.

24...fxg4

A difficult decision which allows White to make the most of his bishop pair. However everything else is bad news for Black. For example: 24...♘h6 25 g5 ♘f7 26 ♘xe6 ♕xe6 27 ♕d4 ♖g8 28 ♕d7 (the dominance of the d-file seals White's advantage) 28...♕xd7 29 ♖xd7 ♖ad8 30 ♖1d4 wins or 24...♖ad8 25 gxf5 ♗xf5 26 ♖g1! beautifully exploiting the exposed queen.

25 ♘xe6 ♕xe6 26 ♕xe4 ♕xe4 27 ♗xe4 gxh3 28 ♖d7

Finally White's control of the d-file pays dividends because the rook on the seventh rank is poised to grab as much material as possible.

28...♖ad8 29 ♖1d3 ♖de8 30 ♖xh3 h6 31 ♗g6!

The most precise continuation, illustrating his python-like grip on the position. Alternatively 31 ♖xb7 allows 31...♗f6! giving Black some hopes of survival.

31...♔g8 32 ♖e3

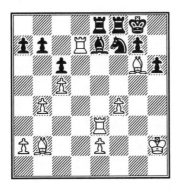

1-0

SUMMARY

The game **Van Wely-Guliev** is a heavyweight encounter which demonstrates how effective a rapid advance on the queenside can be. Black rushes into a typical kingside attack but his lack of reinforcements allows White to show the flaws in this impetuous plan. White tends to hold a space advantage in lines with 6 b4 but in practice it is not always obvious how to exploit this. **Schandorff-Glienke** is a good example of how the bishop pair can exert considerable influence on the board. **Mikhalchishin-Kavcić** is another illustration of a queenside pawn advance by White and a noteworthy example of how the combination of ♘bd2 and c2-c4 can provide an effective challenge to Black's centre.

Macieja-Lesiège shows an unusual way of dealing with the Classical Dutch: White develops his queen's bishop to f4 and then seeks to advantageously open the c-file for his queen's rook. It works wonders here because White not only picks up a pawn but is able to follow up with a stunning king-hunt. **Romanishin-Spinelli** sees the intriguing 6 ♗e5 which should perplex most opponents. Once again White's opening plan is easy to remember and simple to execute: fast development and a swift opening of the c-file. Finally, the Ilyin-Zhenevsky System comes under scrutiny in **Biriukov-Vager** where White follows the usual strategy of rapidly advancing the b-pawn to gain space on the queenside.

THE BENONI

HISTORY OF THE ANTI-BENONI

After years of trying to keep up with the latest theoretical innovations against the Benoni many players have decided to cut their workload by adopting the move-order 1 d4 ♘f6 2 ♘f3 c5 3 d5. Now, as long as White avoids playing c2-c4, he will keep the game in the channels of his desired anti-Benoni line whereas Black will find himself on unfamiliar ground. By dictating the game in this way White has every chance of gaining an opening advantage and Black's detailed knowledge of his favourite opening will be made redundant.

IDEAS BEHIND THE OPENING

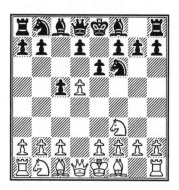

This is considered the main alternative because Black is relying on the continuation 4 c4 exd5 5 cxd5 d6 6 ♘c3 g6 with a standard Benoni. However 4 ♘c3 avoids the heavily analysed lines and White enters the relatively little known anti-Benoni line. In this case, Black usually exchanges on d5 when it is up to White to prove whether his space advantage is enough to maintain the initiative or whether he should start an attack on the kingside. Other ideas for Black are to try 3...d6 or sometimes 3...g6, which tend to transpose to the same line of the Schmid Benoni. The idea is to develop behind a wall of black pawns and then gradually unravel the pieces.

HOW TO BEAT THE BENONI

In the first game I look at a main line of the anti-Benoni where I suggest a fairly safe idea which requires a basic understanding of how to play the middlegame. Black makes the customary exchange on d5 but this is fairly harmless and as there are few tactics for White to worry about he will come out of the opening safely and with confidence.

After 1 d4 ♘f6 2 ♘f3 c5 3 d5 e6 4 ♘c3 Black can try 4...b5 but White replies 5 ♗g5 when knowledge of the similar anti-Benko system should allow White to emerge from the opening with a slight edge. There are various obscure alternatives after 3...d6 but these are covered later on in the chapter to save White walking into the unknown. In the Schmid Benoni after 1 d4 ♘f6 2 ♘f3 c5 3 d5 g6 4 ♘c3 ♗g7 5 e4 d6 White should test the trendy idea 6 ♗b5+.

Basically this avoids the standard lines with 6 ♗e2 and gives Black something extra to think about.

Dautov-Miezis
Bad Zwesten 1997

1 d4 ♘f6 2 ♘f3 c5 3 d5 e6 4 ♘c3

This is my suggestion to avoid the main lines of the Benoni that occur after 4 c4.

4...exd5

The enterprising gambit 4...b5 is discussed in the next main game.

5 ♘xd5 ♘xd5 6 ♕xd5

In the first few moves, White has been granted an advantage in both development and space. However strong players of the black pieces are able to create an appropriate defensive barrier, which requires patience to break down.

6...♗e7

Miezis prepares quick kingside castling to protect his pawn on f7.

Also possible:

a) 6...♘c6 7 e4 d6 8 ♗c4 ♗e6 9 ♕d3 and now:

a1) 9...♗e7 10 c3 ♗xc4 11 ♕xc4 ♕d7 12 ♕d5 ♕e6 (Black is rightly wary of having to defend his backward d-pawn and seeks to simplify matters) 13 ♗f4 ♕xd5 14 exd5 ♘b8 15 0-0-0 ♘a6 16 ♘d2 ♔d7 17 ♖he1 ♘c7 18 ♘e4 when White's space advantage gives him an edge, Miton-Manolov, Cannes 2000.

a2) 9...♘b4 10 ♕e2 (10 ♗b5+ ♔e7 11 ♕e2 ♘xc2+! 12 ♕xc2 ♕a5+ 13 ♗d2 ♕xb5 gave Black the advantage in Kasparov-Illescas Cordoba, Madrid 1988, even though White eventually won) 10...♗xc4 11 ♕xc4 d5 12 exd5 ♕xd5 13 ♕xd5 ♘xd5 14 ♗g5! (14 ♗d2 is the old move but White wants to provoke Black) 14...f6 15 0-0-0 ♖d8 16 ♗d2 with roughly equal chances, B.Gulko-Szmetan, Cali 2001.

b) 6...d6 7 e4 ♘c6 transposes to line 'a' in this note.

7 e4 ♘c6 8 ♗c4

A consistent approach which echoes the sub-variation where the light-squared bishop comes to c4 to add pressure to f7. The quiet option 8 ♗e2 was explored in Karpov-Topalov, Dos Hermanas 1994, which went 8...0-0 9 0-0 d6 10 c3 (simply to stop 10...♘b4) 10...♗e6 11 ♕h5 h6 12 ♖d1 ♖e8 13 ♗f4 ♗f8! with equal chances.

8...0-0 9 0-0 d6

If Black pushes the queen away with 9...♘b4 then 10 ♕d1 is a safe choice intending c2-c3. However, I rather like 10 ♕h5 when 10...♘xc2 allows White to create a strong initiative after 11 ♘g5! ♗xg5 12 ♗xg5 ♕e8 13 ♖ad1 ♘d4 14 ♕h4 threatening ♗e7 with the advantage.

10 c3

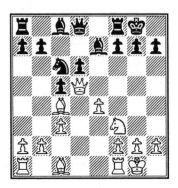

Dautov takes precautions to rule out the possibility of ….♘b4 or even …♘d4 at a later stage of the game. Another approach was seen in the game Pedersen-Miezis, Morso 2002, where White tried to create kingside attacking chances by 10 ♕h5. That game went 10…♗e6 11 ♘g5!? (11 ♗xe6 fxe6 12 ♕g4 ♖f6 13 ♖d1 is a more correct way to gain the advantage) 11…♗xg5 12 ♗xg5 ♕d7 13 ♗xe6 ♕xe6 14 ♖ae1? ♕xa2 and Black got away with grabbing the pawn and eventually converted the extra material into victory.

10...♗e6

It is understandable that Black is in no mood to allow the white queen to dominate the board. A couple of alternatives have been tested:

a) 10…♗g4 11 ♗f4! (White is content to allow the f-pawns to be doubled because Black cannot easily exploit the situation and there is still pressure against the pawn on d6. Instead 11 ♕d3 is met by 11…♔h8 intending …f7-f5 with decent play) 11…♗xf3 12 gxf3 ♘e5 13 ♗xe5 dxe5 14 ♖ad1 ♕b6?! (14…♕c7 preserves the e-pawn although 15 ♕d7 gives White a slight edge) 15 ♕xe5 ♖ae8 16 ♖d7 ♕g6+ 17 ♕g3 when Black has nothing to show for the pawn, Clara-Loeffler, German Team Championship 1990.

b) 10…♘a5 (the obvious threat is 11…♗e6) 11 ♗d3 g6 (White must watch out for 12…♗e6 which would now trap his queen) 12 ♗c2 ♗e6 13 ♕d2 ♗f6 (13…♘c4 14 ♕h6 ♗f6?! 15 ♘g5! is good for White) 14 ♕f4 (14 ♕h6 is not so effective when faced with 14…♗g7) 14…♘c4 15 ♕g3 ♗g7 16 ♘g5 ♘e5 17 ♗f4 ♕e7 18 ♘xe6 ♕xe6 19 ♖fd1 (not 19 ♖ad1? when 19…♕xa2 wins a pawn) 19…c4 20 ♖d2, intending to double rooks and gang up against the weak backward d-pawn, gave White the advantage in Karpov-Kouvatsou, Rethymno 2001.

11 ♕d3 ♕d7 12 ♗f4 ♖ad8 13 ♖ad1 ♔h8

Black puts his king in the corner so as to prepare ...f7-f5. After the immediate 13...f5 White should be able to retain an endgame advantage by 14 ♗xe6+ ♕xe6 15 ♕d5 ♕xd5 16 exd5 ♘a5 17 ♖fe1 ♖fe8 (or 17...♗f6?! 18 ♖e6 ♘c4 19 b3 ♘b2 20 ♖d2 ♗xc3 21 ♖c2 ♘d3 22 ♗xd6 wins) 18 ♖e6 b5?! (18...h6 is necessary when 19 ♖de1 ♔f7 20 h4 offers White the better chances) 19 ♖de1 ♔f7 20 ♗g5! ♗f6 21 ♗xf6 gxf6 22 ♘h4 winning. Alternatively 13...♗xc4 does little to reduce the pressure on the d-file after 14 ♕xc4 ♕e6 15 ♕d5 ♕xd5 when the difference from the previous note is that 16 ♖xd5 is now possible after which doubling rooks is the next step to help win the d6 pawn.

14 ♖fe1!

Dautov sets a little positional trap in view of Black's obvious plan.

14...f5?!

Perhaps 14...h6 should be considered although 15 ♗g3 f5 16 ♗xe6 ♕xe6 17 ♕d5 maintains White's initiative.

15 ♘g5!

This is the star move that White was counting on. Black is now obliged to go in for a losing combination.

15...♗xc4

If 15...♗xg5 then White is on top after 16 ♗xg5 ♖de8 (16...♘e5? 17 ♗xe6 ♕xe6 18 exf5 wins) 17 ♗xe6 ♕xe6 (17...♖xe6? 18 exf5 ♖xe1+ 19 ♖xe1 ♖xf5? 20 ♕xf5! wins) 18 ♕xd6 ♕xd6 19 ♖xd6 fxe4 20 ♖d7.

16 ♕xc4 ♗xg5

The threats of ♘e6 and ♘f7+, forking the rooks, force Black's response.

17 ♗xg5

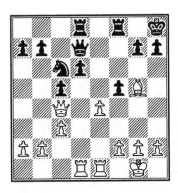

17...♖de8?

What else? 17...♘e7 is hopeless after 18 exf5 uncovering a discovered attack on the knight. And 17...♘e5 still leaves Black under intense pressure after 18 ♕d5 which exploits White's tactics on the d-file. For instance: 18...♖de8 19 f4 ♘g6 (19...♘f7 20 e5!) 20 exf5 (White is spoilt for choice because 20 e5 is also good) 20...♖xe1+ 21 ♖xe1 ♖xf5 22 ♕e6 ♕xe6 23 ♖xe6 (the active rook is a menace to the black pawns) 23...d5 24 ♖d6 ♔g8 25 ♖d8+ ♔f7 26 g4 wins.

18 ♕xc5

At last the rook on the d-file pays dividends in the form of an extra pawn.

18...♖e5 19 ♕xd6 ♕xd6 20 ♖xd6 f4

Of course 20...fxe4 recovers a pawn but after 21 ♗e3 accurate play should result in a win for White who still has an extra pawn.

21 ♖d5 h6 22 ♖xe5 ♘xe5 23 ♗e7 ♖e8 24 ♗d6 ♘d3 25 ♖e2 ♘c1

The black knight is about to run out of escape squares but 25...♖d8 allows a routine victory after 26 ♗c7 ♖c8 27 ♖d2.

26 ♖c2 1-0

Another ploy for Black is to avoid simplification by exchanging on d5 and trying to complicate matters with 4...b5.

De Wachter-Liardet
World Student Championship, Rotterdam 1998

1 d4 ♘f6 2 ♘f3 c5 3 d5 e6 4 ♘c3 b5!?

Black endeavours to make the most of the absence of a white pawn on c4.

5 ♗g5

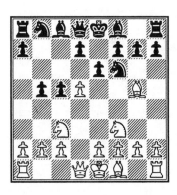

White pins the king's knight in order to help protect his d-pawn. Although White can win a pawn with 5 dxe6 fxe6 6 ♘xb5 I do not think this is appropriate for our proposed repertoire as White cannot steer the game towards the desired middlegame because it is Black who has a lead in development and the initiative. For example: 6...♕a5+ 7 ♘c3 d5 (the blatant threat is 8...d4 to win the queen's knight) 8 e3 ♗d6 9 ♗d2 ♕d8 10 ♗b5+ ♘bd7 11 ♘g5 ♖b8 12 ♕e2 ♕e7 13 ♗a6 ♗xa6 14 ♕xa6 0-0 15 b3 c4 16 ♘f3 ♘c5 0-1 Ottmani-Marzolo, Val Thorens 1998.

5...b4

Or 5...♕a5?! 6 ♗xf6 gxf6 7 ♘d2 is better for White because he has managed to double the f-pawns and easily blocked any tactics associated with the pin on e1-a5 diagonal.

6 ♘e4

I like this simple idea of putting pressure on the knight on f6. Instead 6 ♘a4!? requires careful handling as the knight on the side of the board is temporarily poorly placed. For instance: 6...♕a5 7 ♗xf6 gxf6 8 b3 f5 9 e3 led to equal chances in Sakaev-Volkov, FIDE World Ch 2000.

6...♗b7

The natural 6...♗e7 can be cleverly exploited by 7 d6! ♘xe4 8 ♗xe7 ♕b6 9 ♘e5 ♘c6 (9...♗b7 10 e3 a5? 11 ♕h5! g6 12 ♕h6 gives White a winning position) 10 ♘xc6 ♕xc6 11 f3 ♘f6 12 e4 with the better chances as Black has the problem of whisking his king to safety, Prosviriakov-Alburt, New York 1991.

7 c4

White wishes to retain the tension in the centre by supporting the d5-pawn. If White is looking for a possible alternative then he might consider 7 ♗xf6, which was played in Philippe-Balogh, Dortmund 2001. That game went 7...gxf6 8 c4 f5 9 ♘g3 (White intends e2-e4 to weaken the black pawns and develop the king's bishop) 9...♕f6 10 ♖b1 ♖g8 11 e4 fxe4 12 ♘xe4 ♕g6 13 ♗d3 f5 (13...♕xg2? 14 ♘f6+ ♔d8 15 ♖g1 ♕xg1+ 16 ♘xg1 ♖xg1+ 17 ♗f1 is better for White) 14 ♘g3 with roughly equal chances.

7...bxc3

The decision to break the pin by 7...♗e7 is not convincing after 8 ♗xf6. For instance:

a) 8...♗xf6?! allows White to grab the advantage by 9 ♘d6+ ♔e7 10 ♘xb7 ♕b6 11 ♘xc5 ♕xc5 12 ♕d2 (12 ♕b3 a5 13 ♖d1 is also good for White) 12...♕xc4 13 d6+ ♔e8 when Black is suffering because forfeiting the right to castle has left his pieces in a state of disharmony.

b) 8...gxf6 9 ♘g3 f5 10 ♕d2 a5 11 e4 (White wisely probes the weak black pawn structure in order to optimise his active knights) 11...fxe4 12

♘xe4 f5 13 ♘g3 h5 14 h4 (White makes sure the h5-pawn cannot advance, leaving it a soft target) 14...♗f6 15 0-0-0 a4 16 ♔b1 a3 17 b3 ♗g7 18 ♕g5 (naturally White dare not allow Black to put his queen on the a1-h8 diagonal so is willing to enter a favourable ending) 18...♕f6 19 ♕xf6 ♗xf6 20 ♗e2 ♘a6 21 ♘g5 with a clear advantage because the black h-pawn will soon leave the board, Goldin-Ruiz, Philadelphia 1999.

8 ♘xc3 ♕a5

Or 8...exd5 9 ♗xf6 ♕xf6 10 ♘xd5 ♗xd5 11 ♕xd5 ♕xb2 12 ♖d1 c4 {12...♕c3+ 13 ♖d2 ♕a1+ 14 ♖d1 ♕c3+ is equal although 15 ♘d2, intending e2-e3 and ♗c4, has been suggested} 13 ♕e4+ ♔d8 14 ♕xc4 led to complications slightly favouring White, Sorri-Porrasmaa, Finland Team Ch 1994.

9 ♗xf6 gxf6 10 e4 f5?

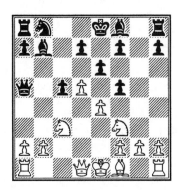

Liardet thinks that White's central pawns need to be undermined but this is too risky due to the severe weakening of the black pawn structure.

11 dxe6

Not 11 exf5?! when 11...♗xd5 justifies Black's set-up.

11...fxe6

11...dxe6 also leaves Black struggling to cope with an exposed king after 12 exf5 ♗g7 13 ♕d2 ♗xf3 (13...exf5 is well met by 14 ♘h4) 14 gxf3 0-0 15 ♖g1 (a simple but effective attacking device to put pressure on the g-file) 15...♔h8 16 ♖xg7! ♔xg7 17 f6+ ♔xf6 (17...♔h8 18 ♕h6 ♖g8 19 ♗d3) 18 ♘e4+ ♔e7 19 ♕xa5 winning.

12 ♘e5

Look out for the threat of ♕h5+. The opening has been a complete triumph for White.

12...h5 13 ♗e2

White reinforces the threat to the h5 square and inevitably the black position will buckle under the strain.

13...♖g8 14 ♗xh5+ ♔d8 15 ♘f7+ ♔c7 16 ♕d2

A quiet move which complements the earlier lightning attack. White wants to add the queen's rook to the onslaught.

16...♕b6 17 0-0-0 ♖xg2

Black tries his luck by capturing some material but his miserable development and poorly placed king spells doom.

18 exf5 exf5 19 ♖he1

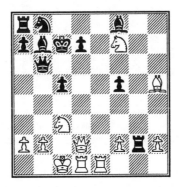

Another rook is added to the attack and now the threat is ♖e8.

19...d6 20 ♘xd6! ♗xd6 21 ♘b5+ ♔c6

There is not much choice considering that 21...♔d7 is met by 22 ♕xd6+ ♕xd6 23 ♖xd6+ ♔c8 24 ♖e8 mate.

22 ♗e8+ ♘d7 23 ♗xd7+ 1-0

White can avoid playing c2-c4 in the opening against whatever set-up that Black plays. In the next example a host of alternatives on move four are examined but none are particularly threatening for White.

Veingold-Nyysti
Naantali 1999

1 d4 ♘f6 2 ♘f3 c5 3 d5 d6

Black is hoping for 4 c4 so that he can transpose to one of the familiar lines in the Benko or the Benoni. He will be disappointed. It is worth remembering that 3...g6 tends to transpose to the next main game after 4 ♘c3 ♝g7 5 e4 d6 (otherwise White plays 6 e5 with advantage) and now 6 ♝b5+ transposes to Aseev-Alekseev.

4 ♘c3

4...♕a5?!

The queen comes out to pin the queen's knight in order to facilitate ...b7-b5. The usual move is 4...g6, which is discussed in the next game. Others:

a) 4...♝f5 is played to deter e2-e4 but is fails to do the job properly: 5 ♘d2 ♕a5 (5...g5 was played in Hoffmann-Maus, German Team Ch 1990, which merely weakened the kingside pawn structure: 6 e4 ♝g6 7 ♝d3 ♘bd7 8 ♘c4 h6 9 0-0 a6 10 a4 ♖b8 11 a5 with a grip on the position) 6 ♘c4 ♕c7 7 f3 e6 8 ♝f4 e5 9 ♝g5 ♘bd7 10 e4 ♝g6 11 a4 a6 12 a5 when White has closed down the queenside, stopping any significant counterplay, and has a space advantage, Brenninkmeijer-Armas, Sonnevanck 1995.

b) 4...e6 5 dxe6 and now:

b1) 5...fxe6 6 e4 d5 7 ♝g5 (the pin on the knight immediately gives Black problems defending d5) 7...♝e7 8 ♝b5+ ♘c6 9 exd5 exd5 10 0-0 (10 ♘e5 ♕d6 11 ♝f4 also looks good for White) 10...0-0 11 ♝xf6 ♝xf6 12 ♕xd5+ ♕xd5 13 ♘xd5 ♝g4 (Black cannot grab a pawn with 13...♝xb2? because of 14 ♖ab1 ♝f6 15 ♘c7 ♖b8 16 ♝xc6 winning) 14 ♘xf6+ ♖xf6 15 ♝xc6 bxc6 16 ♘e5 led to a winning endgame in Gaya Yodra-Romero Leon, Mallorca 2001.

b2) 5...♝xe6 6 e4 ♝e7 7 ♝b5+ ♘c6 (7...♝d7 is a solid reply when 8 a4 is slightly better for White) 8 e5 ♘d5 (or 8...dxe5 9 ♕xd8+ ♖xd8 10 ♘xe5 ♝d7 11 ♝xc6 ♝xc6 12 ♘xc6 bxc6 13 0-0 with a small edge due to Black's doubled c-pawns) 9 ♘xd5 ♝xd5 10 ♕xd5 ♕a5+ 11 c3 ♕xb5 12 exd6 ♖d8 13 a4 ♕b6 14 ♝f4 gave White the superior chances, Stohl-Bistric, Pula 1999.

c) 4...e5 5 e4 ♗e7 (after 5...g6 White should play in the same style as the main game Aseev-Alekseev with 6 ♗b5+ when play might continue 6... ♘bd7 7 a4 a6 8 ♗e2 b6 9 0-0 ♗g7 10 ♘d2 0-0 11 ♘c4 giving White the slightly better chances) 6 ♗b5+ ♘bd7 7 a4 (White is wary of allowing ...a7-a6 because when the bishop retreats ...b7-b5 is possible) 7...0-0 8 0-0 ♘e8 9 ♗d3 ♔h8 10 ♘e2 g6 11 ♗h6 ♘g7 12 ♘d2 with roughly equal chances, Ekeberg-T. Hansen, Gausdal 2002.

5 ♗d2!

The bishop move has been shown to the best reply having helped White to a number of victories. 5 ♘d2?! is not so convincing because after 5...b5 the c4 square is denied to the knight. The game Gavritenkov-Skytte, Tula 2000, continued 6 e4 b4 (6...a6 7 a4 b4 8 ♘cb1 g6 9 ♗e2 ♕c7 10 b3 (10 c3!? is probably worth testing) 10...♗g7 11 ♗b2 0-0 12 0-0 e6 13 dxe6 ♗xe6 14 ♗d3 d5 gave Black the edge in Gonda-Fogarasi, Budapest 2002) 7 ♘cb1 g6 8 b3 ♗g7 9 ♗b2 0-0 10 ♘c4 ♕c7 11 ♘bd2 e6 12 e5 dxe5 13 ♗xe5 ♕d8 14 d6 ♗b7 (White may have acquired a passed pawn but without sufficient piece back-up this is a hollow victory. Now the useful bishop on b7 targets g2, stopping White from comfortably developing his kingside) 15 a3 ♘bd7 16 ♗b2 a5 17 c3 ♘d5! (enabling the king's bishop to make an impact on the long diagonal) 18 cxb4 ♗xb2 19 ♘xb2 ♘c3 20 ♕g4 ♕f6 21 ♗d3 ♘d5 22 ♖b1 ♘f4 23 bxc5 ♘xc5 0-1.

5...b5

The only move that makes sense after the previous queen move.

6 ♘e4 ♕b6

The queen retreats and keeps guard on the b-pawn.

Alternatives are:

a) 6...♕c7?! 7 ♘xf6+ exf6 8 e4 a6 9 c4 (9 a4 is also possible with similar play to the main game) 9...♕e7 10 ♕c2 b4 11 a3 b3 12 ♕xb3 ♕xe4+ 13 ♗e2 ♗e7 14 0-0 0-0 (or 14...♕xe2 15 ♖fe1 when the black queen has no escape squares) 15 ♖fe1 ♕f5 16 ♘h4 ♕d7 (Black has wasted a lot of time moving his queen with the result that his queenside pieces are still on their original squares) 17 ♕g3 ♗d8? (17...♔h8 at least avoids an instant loss but after 18 ♗d3 g6 19 ♗c3 White still has a dangerous attack) 18 ♗h6 g6 19 ♗d3 f5 (19...♖e8 20 ♘xg6! hxg6 21 ♗xg6 fxg6 22 ♕xg6+ ♔h8 22 ♖xe8+ wins) 20 ♘xf5 ♗f6 21 ♗xf8 ♔xf8 22 ♘xd6 1-0 Garcia Ilundain-Bellon Lopez, Santa Clara 1998.

b) 6...♕a4?! has been played but Black would need a lot courage to place his queen on a square where one slip would allow it to be trapped: 7 ♘xf6+ exf6 8 e3 ♘d7 (8...a6 takes away a possible emergency escape square for the queen, e.g. 9 ♗d3 ♕g4 {9...c4? allows White to exploit the position of the black queen with 10 b3! ♕a3 11 bxc4 bxc4 12 ♗xc4)} 10 h3 ♕h5 11 c4 with the brighter prospects due to the better development and the fact that the black queen is not yet completely safe) 9 b3 ♕e4 10 ♗xb5 ♕xd5 11 0-0 ♕b7 (just count the number of times the black queen has moved and it is clear that he must be behind in development) 12 ♗d3 ♗e7 (12...♘e5 might allow Black to untangle his doubled pawns after 13 ♘xe5 fxe5 but White has a pleasant game especially with his strong bishop aimed at h7—and after 14 c4 e4 15 ♗c2 ♗e7 16 ♗c3 0-0 17 ♕h5 White intends f2-f3 with a strong attack) 13 c4 ♕c6 14 b4 ♗b7 (Black is grateful to get another piece into the action but he should probably hold back for a moment. Instead 14...cxb4?! 15 ♘d4 ♕c5 16 ♕g4! g6 17 ♕e4 d5 18 ♕xd5 gives White a clear advantage but 14...a6 is a safer choice) 15 b5 ♕c7 16 e4 0-0 17 a4, with the intention of pushing the a-pawn, gave White a good position in Dautov-Mainka, Munster 1997.

7 ♘xf6+ exf6 8 e4!

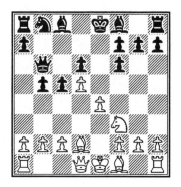

White already has a comfortable game because he has the simple plan of undermining the queenside pawns followed by developing his kingside.

8...a6

If 8...♗e7 then, as in the main game, 9 c3 is played to allow White to take back with the queen after a2-a4. For instance: 9...f5 (Black wishes to rid himself of the doubled f-pawns but 9...0-0 is worthy of attention) 10 exf5 ♗xf5 11 a4 bxa4 12 ♕xa4+ ♗d7 (or else 12...♘d7 13 ♗b5 ♖b8 14 c4 is good for White) 13 ♕c2 0-0 14 ♗d3 (as usual the position is easier for White to play because he has more room to develop and has attacking chances on the kingside) 14...h6 15 0-0 ♗f6 16 ♗f4 ♕c7 17 ♘d2 (a theme of these lines is that if a knight comes to c4 then the d6 pawn is usually under a lot of strain—as is the case here) 17...♗g5 18 ♗xg5 hxg5 19 f4 g4 20 f5 f6 21 ♖f4 gave White a clear advantage Burmakin-Baklan, Graz 1997.

9 c3 g6

The kingside fianchetto is understandable because the bishop on g7 will apply pressure on the long diagonal after an eventual ...f6-f5.

10 a4 bxa4 11 ♕xa4+ ♗d7 12 ♕c2

A quiet move to defend b2 but the damage has already been done—the a6 pawn is weak and the bishop on d7 misplaced because it stops Black's queen's knight getting out.

12...♗g7 13 ♗f4 0-0 14 ♗d3 ♖d8 15 0-0

Veingold has just got on with the job of developing—something which is not so easy for Black.

15...♗b5 16 ♕b3!

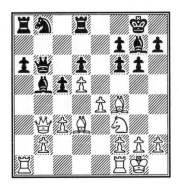

A tricky move that rebuffs Black's hopes of a peaceful exchange. Now the big threat is 17 c4 winning the pinned bishop.

16...♕b7 17 ♘d2

Defending the queen and so renewing the threat of c3-c4. If an immediate 17 c4 then of course 17...♗c6 saves the piece.

17...♖a7

17...♕d7? is hopeless after 18 ♗xb5 ♕xb5 19 ♕xb5 axb5 20 ♖xa8.

18 ♗xb5 axb5 19 ♖xa7 ♕xa7 20 ♕xb5

White is a clear pawn up and soon b2-b4 will produce a strong passed pawn.

20...♗f8 21 ♘c4 ♖d7 22 ♘a5 ♕a6 23 ♕xa6 ♘xa6 24 ♖a1 1-0

Black resigns prematurely but the position is lost because White has active pieces and can create a strong passed pawn.

Probably the best course of action for Black is kingside castling in conjunction with a kingside fianchetto. I recommend 6 ♗b5+, which is the latest twist in White's attempt to wrest the initiative from Black.

Aseev-Alekseev

St Petersburg 2000

1 d4 ♘f6 2 ♘f3 c5 3 d5 d6 4 ♘c3 g6 5 e4 ♗g7 6 ♗b5+

I have changed the move-order slightly for ease of reference but the game originally started 1 d4 c5 (see the Odd Openings chapter for more details on this move, but play usually transposes...) 2 d5 d6 3 e4 ♘f6 4 ♘c3 g6 5 ♘f3 ♗g7 6 ♗b5+!?

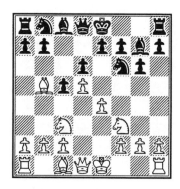

An annoying check for Black because it poses a fresh set of problems in comparison to the main line with 6 ♗e2 and takes players out of their opening theory. This is because the check needs to be blocked but the obvious 6...♘bd7 denies Black the usual development of the queen's knight to a6 and c7 where it usefully supports an advance of the b-pawn.

6...♘bd7

a) 6...♗d7 7 a4 0-0 8 0-0 when play might continue:

a1) 8...♗g4 9 ♖e1 (9 h3!? is a decent alternative) 9...a6 10 ♗f1 e5 11 dxe6 (once again 11 h3 should be considered) 11...fxe6 12 ♗e2 ♘c6 (now that White has exchanged on e6 the c6 square is available for the queen's knight) 13 ♗e3 ♖b8 14 h3 ♗xf3 15 ♗xf3 ♘e8 16 ♗e2 ♘c7 with equal chances. Orso-Yu Mingyuan, Budapest 2001.

a2) 8...♘a6 is part of an elaborate manoeuvre to help support the advance of the b-pawn: 9 ♖e1 (after 9 ♗xa6 bxa6 Black has sufficient compensation for the doubled a-pawns after his rook occupies the semi-open b-file) 9...♘c7 10 ♗f1 ♖b8 11 h3 a6 12 ♗f4 (now that Black can advance the b-pawn with impunity White switches his attention to the centre) 12...♘h5 13 ♗h2 ♘e8 14 e5! and White had an edge in Rytshagov-Kulaots, Rakvere 2000.

b) 6...♘fd7 is a favourite with those who do not want their standard plan of ...♘b8-a6-c7 to be disrupted: 7 a4 (as usual this move is important because it deters ...a7-a6 followed by ...b7-b5) 7...0-0 8 0-0 ♘a6 9 ♖e1 (9 ♗f4 ♘c7 10 ♗c4 is a reasonable alternative) 9...♘c7 10 ♗f1 a6 11 ♗f4 ♖b8 12 a5 b5 13 axb6 ♘xb6 14 h3 ♗b7 15 ♕d2 with roughly equal chances, Kononenko-Calzetta, Varna 2002.

7 a4

A precaution against Black's ...a7-a6 and ...b7-b5, mobilising the queen-side pawns.

7...0-0 8 0-0 a6 9 ♗e2 b6 10 ♖e1

10 h3 is also possible with the idea of continuing ♗f4 and meeting ...♘h5 with a retreat to h2: 10...♗b7 11 ♗f4 ♘e8 12 ♕d2 e5?! 13 dxe6 fxe6 14 ♖ad1 (White already has a promising game due to the pressure against the d6 pawn) 14...♘df6 15 ♘g5! (or 15 ♗xd6 ♘xd6 16 ♕xd6 ♕xd6 17 ♖xd6 ♘xe4 is not so clear) 15...e5 16 ♗xe5 ♘xe4 17 ♗c4+ d5 18 ♘cxe4 ♗xe5 19 ♘e6 led to a winning advantage in Gasanov-Kislinsky, Kharkov 2001.

10...♘e8

The start of a manoeuvre to help support the advance of the b-pawn. It is by no means obvious and so at this point many Black players fail to find a convincing plan to revitalise their passive position. 10...♖b8 is also designed to support ...b6-b5, e.g. 11 ♗f1 ♕c7 12 ♗f4 ♘e5 13 h3 ♘xf3+ 14 ♕xf3 ♘d7 15 ♖ad1 with a slight edge for White, Wells-Conquest, Oakham 1994.

11 ♗g5

The bishop is developed and as a bonus it pins the e-pawn.

11...♘c7 12 ♘d2 ♖b8 13 ♘c4

Another idea associated with 11 ♗g5 is revealed—the threat of ♘xd6.

13...♘e5

13...b5 is a critical continuation but White has prepared for such an eventuality and can continue with 14 ♘xd6! b4 (14...f6 15 ♘xc8 fxg5 16 ♘a7 with a clear advantage) 15 ♘xc8 ♕xc8 16 ♘a2 ♗xb2 17 ♗xe7 ensuring an advantage.

14 ♘e3

Aseev avoids the exchange and prepares f2-f4 to drive away the central-ised knight on e5.

14...h6 15 ♗h4 f5?!

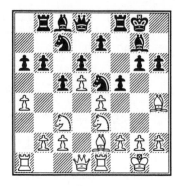

Black has an awkward and cramped position and it is understandable that Alekseev is not content to just patiently sit and wait—so he strikes out at White's centre. However the problem with this thrust is that it weakens his kingside so perhaps instead 15...b5!? should be considered.

16 f4 ♘f7?

Alekseev has spotted a clever plan but unfortunately does not notice that there is a big hole in his analysis. 16...♘g4 represents the best chance although after 17 ♘xg4 fxg4 18 ♕d2 White has a small advantage due to his superiority in space.

17 exf5 ♗d4

Black has little choice but to keep to his plan because 17...gxf5 leaves the f5 pawn vulnerable, e.g. 18 ♗d3 ♘h8 19 ♕h5 ♕e8 20 ♕xe8 ♖xe8 21 ♘xf5 and White has a great ending with an extra pawn.

18 ♗d3 ♘h8

18...♗xf5 is not much help after 19 ♗xf5 gxf5 20 ♕h5 ♕d7 21 ♕g6+ ♔h8 22 ♔h1 ♗xe3 (otherwise White will just take on f5) 23 ♖xe3 ♖be8 24 ♖xe7! ♕xe7 (24...♖xe7 25 ♗f6 mate) 25 ♗xe7 ♖xe7 26 ♕f6+ wins.

19 ♔h1 gxf5

It seems that Black has managed to unbalance the position but his exposed kingside serves as a trigger for a decisive combination.

20 ♘xf5! ♖xf5 21 ♖xe7

This is the twist in the combination which Black had failed to appreciate. Now if the black rook seeks safety by 21...♖f8 then 22 ♗h7 mate is a shocker! And so White remains with a strong rook on the seventh rank against a dangerously exposed black king.

21...♗f6 22 ♖xc7

It is something of a luxury to have two winning continuations but White could also have played 22 ♗xf5 ♕xe7 23 ♗xf6 ♕xf6 24 ♕g4+ ♕g7 25 ♗xc8 when the two pawns advantage is enough to wrap up the game quickly.

22...♖xf4 23 ♗g3 ♖g4 24 ♗h7+ ♔f8

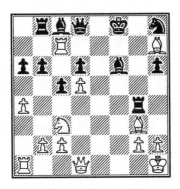

25 ♗xd6+!
A brilliant finish.

25...♕xd6 26 ♖xc8+ ♖xc8 27 ♕xg4 1-0

SUMMARY

If White plays the anti-Benoni line he avoids a lot of opening theory by leaving out the move c2-c4. However he still needs to be on guard against various responses. An examination of one of the main defences in the game **Dautov-Miezis** shows that multiple exchanges can allow White to enter the middlegame with confidence and without falling victim to tricks in the opening. **De Wachter-Liardet** is a great example of how to counter the sharp 4...b5 with strong attacking play and then finish the game in style. The idea of playing an early ...b7-b5 returns in **Veingold-Nyysti** where Black tries 4...♕a5 to support the advance. However this queen sortie is not reckoned to be particularly good and here also it fails to make much of an impression against accurate play. Perhaps Black's best line of defence is that seen in **Aseev-Alekseev**. I believe the trendy 6 ♗b5+ will confuse those players who rely too heavily on old opening books and offer sufficient chances of obtaining the initiative against even the most solid players.

THE PSEUDO-BENKO

When Black tries to take advantage of White's move-order by playing an early ...b7-b5, exploiting the lack of a pawn on c4, we have the Pseudo-Benko. I think White should avoid transposing to main lines and seek an advantage in lesser-known lines which rely predominantly on rapid development.

HISTORY OF THE PSEUDO-BENKO

This opening has been known at international level since Rubinstein-Spielmann, Vienna 1922. Black lost that game and the variation never really caught on, although it was played several times by world championship candidate Paul Keres. The years passed and it continued to be rarely seen until England's first grandmaster Tony Miles jolted the chess world by employing it against Garry Kasparov. However, in a much publicised game, the opening did not prove a success and after his defeat Miles ruefully commented "I thought I was playing a world champion, not a monster with 22 eyes who sees everything". Nevertheless this reverse did not deter a whole host of imitators from trying to find improvements for Black and occasionally the variation was practised by English grandmasters Adams and Hodgson as well as the American Lev Alburt. Nowadays it is regarded as a trendy opening with one of the world's leading players, Bulgarian grandmaster Veselin Topalov, among its fervent supporters.

IDEAS BEHIND THE OPENING

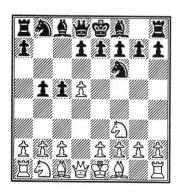

This is the Pseudo-Benko. Black has advanced the b-pawn to take advantage of the fact that White has played neither ♘c3 nor c2-c4 to cover the b5 square. Essentially Black challenges White to enter main lines with 4 c4, transposing to the Benko Gambit Declined. The natural 4 a4 is well met by 4...♗b7 putting pressure on the important central d-pawn. The Benko normally occurs after 1 d4 ♘f6 2 c4 c5 3 d5 b5 so it is clear why Black's formation against our recommended move-order is so appropriately named.

HOW TO BEAT THE PSEUDO-BENKO

It is probably best to avoid entering main lines and having to learn a great deal of complicated opening theory. Far more practical is to play the straightforward 4 ♗g5, as recommended by Kasparov, which has the simple idea of exchanging pieces on f6 to saddle Black with doubled pawns and to allow White to construct a pawn centre with e2-e4.

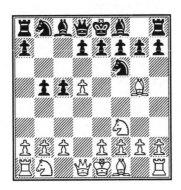

Black's plan will be to undermine the d5 pawn at every opportunity. The simplest way is by fianchettoing the queen's bishop, relying on the fact that any defence of the pawn by ♘c3 can be removed with ...b5-b4, and c2-c4 with ...bxc4. On the other hand, if White manages to support the d5 pawn with e2-e4 then Black can chip away at the centre by ...e7-e6. However stronger players tend to take measures against the doubling of the pawns on f6 before proceeding with any designs against the d5 pawn.

Izeta Txabarri-Bellon Lopez
Leon 1998

1 d4 ♘f6 2 ♘f3 c5 3 d5 b5 4 ♗g5

4...♗b7!?

A natural response, using the newly-vacated b7 square to fianchetto the bishop. It is a rare sight to see a grandmaster resign in 10 moves but that is exactly what happened in Sakaev-Delchev after 4...♕a5+. That game went 5 c3 ♘e4 6 ♗h4 ♗b7!? (6...b4 7 ♕c2 gives White a slight edge) 7 e3 e6? (Black plays routine moves without realising that he is now on the brink of defeat—instead 7...b4 8 c4 e6 9 ♕d3 exd5 10 cxd5 ♘d6 11 ♘bd2 leaves White with an edge in view of the superior co-ordination of his pieces) 8 dxe6 dxe6 (if 8...fxe6 then 9 ♘e5! threatening 10 ♕h5+ is a killer since 9...g6 leads to ruin after 10 ♕f3 ♘d6 11 ♕f6 ♖g8 12 ♗xb5! winning) 9 ♗xb5+ ♘c6 (if 9...♕xb5? 10 ♕d8 mate or 9...♗c6 10 ♗xc6+ ♘xc6 11 ♘bd2 with a clear advantage) 10 ♘e5! 1-0. Black saw that 10...♕c7, defending the mate threat and the queen's knight, fails to 11 ♕a4 winning one of the two simultaneously attacked knights.

5 ♗xf6

The point of White's opening strategy—if given the chance he will double Black's f-pawns.

5...exf6

The obvious capture 5...gxf6?! is frowned upon because then any king-side castling by Black will leave his king exposed. For instance: 6 e4 ♕b6 (the idea of undermining the d5-pawn by 6..f5? is flawed because of 7 exf5 ♗g7 8 c3 ♕b6 9 ♘a3 and Black has no compensation for the pawn) 7 a4 b4 8 a5 ♕d6 9 ♘bd2 (White intends to gain time by chasing the black queen) 9...♗h6 10 ♘c4 ♕f4 11 ♗d3 ♗a6 12 ♕e2 (White gets on with the job of getting his pieces into play—something which is not so easy for Black who is passively placed) 12...♗xc4 13 ♗xc4 0-0 14 g3 ♕g4 15 h3 ♕g7 16 ♘h4 (the knight is heading for the important f5 square and this lures Black into a trap...) 16...e6 17 dxe6 dxe6 18 ♗d5! exd5 19 ♘f5 ♕g5 20 f4 and White wins, Varela-Bulcourf, Buenos Aires 2001.

6 e4

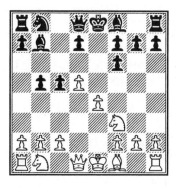

6...a6

The need to defend the b5 pawn has led Black to try a variety of replies:

a) 6...♕e7!? is a direct way of attacking the e-pawn but it tends to congest the kingside: 7 ♘bd2 ♗xd5 (in practice Black rarely compromises his piece development by such pawn-grabbing—alternatively the calm 7...a6 is met by 8 ♗e2 d6 9 0-0 g6 10 a4 with an edge for White) 8 ♗xb5 ♗xe4 9 0-0 ♗d5 10 ♘c4 ♗e6 11 ♕d3 ♘c6 12 c3 ♕d8 (12...g6 seems to be a good idea to further Black's development but after 13 ♖fe1 ♗g7 14 ♘d6+ the black king has to forfeit the right to castle, thereby leaving the rooks in a state of discoordination) 13 ♖fd1 ♕c7 14 ♘e3 ♗e7 15 ♘d5 ♗xd5 16 ♕xd5 ♖d8 (16...0-0? leaves White on top, e.g. 17 ♕xd7 ♖ac8? 18 ♗xc6 ♕xc6 19 ♕xe7 winning) 17 ♘d2 0-0 18 ♘c4 ♖fe8 19 ♖d2 ♗f8 20 ♖ad1 ♘b8 21 ♘e3 ♖e5 22 ♕f3 d6 23 ♘d5 ♕a5 24 a4 ♖c8? 25 ♘xf6+! 1-0 Tangborn-Kuntz, Budapest 1992.

b) 6...c4 is the main alternative:

b1) 7 a4 a6 8 ♘a3?! (the knight on the rim is dim because it cannot exert much pressure on the b5 pawn and so is left misplaced) 8...♕b6 9 ♗e2 ♗c5 10 0-0 0-0 11 a5 ♕a7 12 ♕d2? ♖e8 13 ♕f4 ♗xd5! gave Black an extra pawn in Kurz-Vaganian, German Team Championship 1992.

b2) 7 ♗e2, simply carrying on developing the pieces, is regarded as the best choice: 7...♗c5 8 0-0 a6 9 a4 ♕b6 10 c3 0-0 11 ♘d4 ♖e8 (or 11...♗xd4 12 cxd4 is fine for White because Black's queenside pieces remain passive) 12 ♗f3 d6 13 axb5 axb5 14 ♖xa8 ♗xa8 15 b4 cxb3 (15...♗xd4 16 ♕xd4 ♕xd4 17 cxd4 ♘a6 18 ♘c3 ♘xb4 19 ♘xb5 ♖d8 20 ♖c1 with a superior ending) 16 ♕xb3 ♗xd4 (16...b4? 17 ♕a4! with a winning double attack on the bishop on a8 and rook on e8) 17 cxd4 ♘a6 (or 17...♕xd4 18 ♕xb5 ♖f8 19 ♘a3 when White is better due to Black's poorly placed queenside pieces and weak pawn on d6) 18 ♘a3 with advantage to White, Khalifman-Fominyh, Russian Championship 1995.

7 a4 b4

7...bxa4 releases the tension on the queenside allowing White to manoeuvre more easily thanks to his space advantage. The game Fedorowicz-
Miton, New York 2000, continued 8 ♘c3 d6 9 ♘d2 (with the departure of
the pawn from b5, the king's knight heads for c4) 9...♗e7 10 ♘c4 0-0 11
♗e2 ♘d7 12 ♘xa4 ♕c7 13 0-0 ♖fe8 14 ♗g4 when the threat of ♗xd7 followed by ♘b6 gives White an edge.

8 ♘bd2 d6 9 ♘c4!

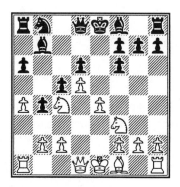

The knight on c4 has a commanding presence and Black will find it very
awkward to get rid of it now that his b-pawn has advanced to b4.

9...♘d7 10 ♗d3 g6

10...a5!? comes into consideration to give Black some room on the
queenside. Play might then proceed 11 0-0 ♗e7 12 ♕d2 with a slight edge.

11 a5! ♘e5?!

11...♗e7 should be preferred if only to keep guard on d6. Then 12 c3
bxc3 13 bxc3 0-0 14 0-0, intending ♖ab1 with similar play to the main
game, gives White the initiative.

12 ♘fxe5 fxe5 13 0-0 ♗e7 14 c3! bxc3

After 14...0-0 White can try 15 cxb4 to isolate the b4 pawn and eventually capture it. For example: 15...cxb4 16 ♘b6 ♖b8 (16...♖a7 17 ♖a4 and
the b-pawn will soon leave the board) 17 ♕e2 and now the a6 pawn is
vulnerable.

15 ♕a4+ ♔f8

15...♕d7? walks into 16 ♕xd7+ ♔xd7 17 ♘b6+ and Black can go home
early.

16 bxc3 ♔g7 17 ♖ab1

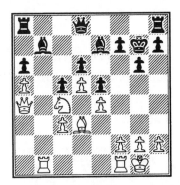

The middlegame plan for White is easy to follow because it involves doubling rooks on the b-file to make life miserable for the bishop on b7, which is hemmed in by White's central pawns.

17...♖a7

Or 17...♖b8 18 ♖b6 ♕c7 19 ♖fb1 when the big threat now is ♕b3 adding even more weight to the pin on the bishop. For instance: 19...♗a8 20 ♕b3 ♖xb6 21 axb6 ♕b7 22 ♘a5 winning.

18 ♖b2 ♗c8 19 ♘b6 f5 20 ♘xc8 ♕xc8 21 ♖b6 fxe4

There is a faint sign of counterplay upon 21...f4 but 22 ♗e2 prevents ...f4-f3, breaking up the kingside pawn structure, allowing White to get on with the job of probing for weaknesses on the queenside.

22 ♕xe4 c4!?

Bellon Lopez is trying to conjure up complications by shedding a pawn. This is hardly surprising because otherwise White will just play ♕e2 intensifying the attack on a6.

23 ♕xc4 ♕xc4 24 ♗xc4 ♖c8 25 ♖c6 ♖ac7

With a material deficit and passive pieces Black has a hopeless ending. There is also no joy in 25...♖xc6 after which 26 dxc6 ♖c7 27 ♗d5 ♗d8 28 ♖b1, intending ♖b6, is winning for White.

26 ♗xa6 ♖xc6 27 dxc6 ♖xc6 28 ♗b5 ♖c7

Black should at least play 28...♖xc3 but the final result is in no doubt. For example: 29 ♖a1 ♖c7 30 a6 ♖a7 31 ♗c6 ♗d8 32 ♗b7 ♗b6 33 ♔f1 and the white rook and king will slowly advance, picking off the black pawns one by one.

29 a6 d5 30 ♖d1 d4 31 cxd4 exd4 32 ♖xd4 1-0

The long-term problem of the doubled f-pawns after White exchanges pieces on f6 has prompted Black to find improvements.

Soln-Velickovic

Slovenian Championship, Grize 2001

1 d4 ♘f6 2 ♘f3 c5 3 d5

3...b5

It is worth mentioning an obscure opening named 'The Hawk' which has been actively promoted by the German openings expert Stefan Bücker and can be instantly recognised by its distinctive 3...c4. However this should not alarm anyone following the repertoire in this book because it is designed to stop c2-c4—which is not part of our opening strategy anyway. Speelman and Shirov have analysed an amazing line that looks very good for White: 4 ♘c3 ♕a5 5 ♕d4!? (for those of you with a nervous disposition and a dislike of intense complications I would highly recommend 5 ♗d2 when 5...♘xd5 6 e4 ♘xc3 7 ♗xc3 ♕c5 8 ♕d4 allows White to restore the material balance with a slight lead in development) 5...♘a6 (5...b5!? 6 e4 ♗b7 7 ♗d2 b4 8 ♘d1 e6 9 ♗xc4 ♗c5 10 ♕d3 0-0 11 ♘e3 gave White the advantage in Volzhin-Rossi, Ohrid 2001) 6 e4 b5!? (This move was suggested by Speelman as an improvement on his game against Paulsen at Hamburg 2000 which continued 6...♘b4 7 ♔d1 e6 8 a3 ♘a6 9 ♗xc4 and the extra pawn can't be bad for White) 7 e5 b4 8 exf6 bxc3 9 fxg7 cxb2+ 10 ♗d2 c3!? (or 10...♗xg7 11 ♕xg7 bxa1=♕+ 12 ♕xa1 c3! 13 ♗xc3 ♘b4 14 ♗d3 0-0 15 0-0 with plenty of room for study although I prefer White because the black king is exposed) 11 gxh8=♕ bxa1=♕+ 12 ♔e2 ♕b5+ 13 ♔e3 ♕b6 (it all looks a complete mess but Shirov is convinced that White is fine) 14 ♕xb6 axb6 15 ♗xc3 ♕c1+ 16 ♘d2 ♘c7 17 ♗g7 ♘xd5+ 18 ♔f3 ♕a3+ 19 ♗d3 e6 20 ♘c4 ♕c5 21 ♗e4 f5 22 ♗xd5 ♕xd5+ 23 ♔g3 f4+ 24

♔h4 ♕c5 25 ♗xf8 ♕xf8 26 ♕xf8+ ♔xf8 27 ♘xb6 with a winning endgame for White.

4 ♗g5 ♕b6

Black chooses a queen development to avoid the doubled pawns. 5 ♗xf6 is now met by 5...♕xf6.

5 a4

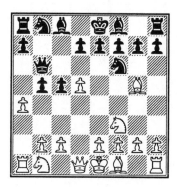

White strikes at once to disturb Black's queenside pawns.

5...bxa4!?

5...♗b7 is an obvious idea to attack the d5 pawn but it fails to impress after 6 axb5! when play might continue:

a) 6...♗xd5 7 ♗xf6 ♗xf3 8 exf3 ♕xf6 (8...♕e6+ is an improvement although 9 ♗e2 exf6 10 ♘c3 is good for White) 9 ♕d5 ♕e6+ 10 ♕xe6 fxe6 11 b6 ♘c6 12 ♗b5 a5 13 ♗xc6 dxc6 14 ♘a3 with a winning ending thanks to the passed b-pawn and Black's weak a-pawn.

b) 6...♘xd5 7 e4 ♘c7 8 ♘c3 a6 9 ♘a4 ♕g6 10 ♘xc5 ♗xe4 11 b6 ♘e6 (not 11...♗xf3?? when 12 bxc7 threatens mate in one and decides the game) 12 ♘xe4 ♕xe4+ 13 ♗e3 g6 14 ♘d2 ♕b7 15 ♘b3 ♘c6 16 ♗c4 1-0 Relange-Prusikhin, Clichy 1998. A sample line reveals why Black resigned at such an early stage of the game. After 16...♗g7 17 ♗xe6 dxe6 18 ♘c5 ♕c8 19 b7 wins. The main alternative is 5...b4, which has the merit of avoiding the sharp lines associated with the main game. 6 a5 (6...♕d6?! 7 ♗xf6 ♕xf6 {7...exf6 8 e4, intending ♘bd2-c4, will demonstrate that the black queen is poorly placed} 8 c3 e6 9 e4 bxc3 10 ♘xc3 d6 11 ♗b5+ ♘d7?! (also 11...♗d7 12 ♕a4 gives White the brighter prospects) 12 ♕b3 e5? 13 ♗c6 1-0 Hjelm-Pera, Jyvaskyla 1999) 6...♕b7 7 ♗xf6 exf6 8 e4 d6 (if Black wishes to fianchetto on the kingside by 8...g6 then 9 ♗d3 ♘g7 10 0-0 0-0 11 ♘bd2 maintains White's space advantage) 9 ♘bd2 ♗e7 10 ♘c4 0-0 11 ♗e2 ♘d7 12 ♘e3 with a slight edge, H.Olafsson-Brynell, Hillerod 1995.

6 ♘c3!?

White intends to capture on a4 with the knight so Black has to accept the challenge of taking another pawn or be left with a passive position.

6...♕xb2 7 ♗d2

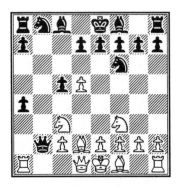

So White has sacrificed two pawns. Why? Well, the pawn on a4 can be recaptured anytime so at the cost of effectively just one pawn White is banking on getting his pieces out quickly—preferably with gain of time by harassing the black queen—and then going for the attack. On the other hand Black believes in his extra pawn and hopes to survive the initial onslaught and eventually convert his material advantage. Having got involved in such a sharp opening it is quite likely that an opponent will later look up the recommended moves in one of the standard reference books. Well, *Modern Chess Openings* does not even mention 3...b5 because White's crafty move-order has side-stepped all the main lines. Admittedly, *Nunn's Chess Openings* does discuss the pawn sacrifices but at this point of the game it stops its analysis with a quote from Bent Larsen stating that the position is 'unclear'. Therefore I believe that this attacking line has every chance of catapulting White to a decisive advantage.

7...♕b6?!

There is some debate as to which square the queen should retreat—but what is certain is that she will soon have to move again! A slight nuance that I have detected is that the odd-looking 7...♕b7 has the benefit of dealing with the plan e2-e4-e5, as carried out in the main game, because at some point the d5 pawn will find itself *en prise* to the joint attack by the queen and king's knight. However, I would be quite impressed if anybody playing Black and new to this position could work all that out and not lose on time in the process! After 7...♕b7 White has plenty of pressure as compensation for the pawn. For example: 8 e4 g6?! (8...d6 looks a sterner test for White when Burgess-L.Christensen, Copenhagen 1992, continued 9 ♖b1 ♕c7 10 ♗c4 ♘bd7 11 ♕e2 a6 12 ♘xa4 g6 13 0-0 ♗g7 14 ♖b3 0-0 15 ♖fb1 ♖b8

16 ♖xb8 ♘xb8 17 h3 ♘fd7 18 ♖b3 ♘e5 19 ♘xe5 ♗xe5 20 f4 ♗g7 21 ♘b6 ♘d7 and now, instead of 23 ♗a5, White should have restored the material balance by 23 ♘xc8 ♖xc8 24 ♗xa6 when the bishop pair gives him an edge) 9 ♖b1 ♕c7 10 e5 ♘g4 11 d6 ♕d8? (a mistake that allows White to complete a brilliant miniature) 12 ♘d5! exd6 13 ♗g5 f6 (13...♕a5+ 14 c3 winning) 14 exf6 ♕a5+ 15 ♘d2 ♘e5 16 ♖b5! 1-0 Piket-J.Polgar, Brussels 1987.

8 e4 d6 9 e5 dxe5 10 ♘xe5 ♘bd7

Velickovíc hopes to ease the pressure by exchanging pieces. Also possible is 10...g6 when 11 ♖b1 ♕c7 12 ♗b5+! ♗d7 13 ♗f4 ♕c8 14 d6 (14 ♘xd7 is also good when 14...♘fxd7 15 ♘xa4 ♗g7 16 ♕f3, threatening 17 d6, is better for White) 14...♗g7 (14...♗xb5 is supposed to be an improvement but after 15 ♘xb5 ♘a6 16 c3, with the idea of 17 ♕xa4, leaves Black in disarray) 15 dxe7 a6 16 ♘c4 axb5 17 ♘d6+ ♔xe7 18 ♘xc8+ ♖xc8 19 ♕d6+ ♔d8 20 ♘d5 gives White a winning advantage, Vyzhmanavin-Arbakov, Moscow 1986.

11 ♗b5 g6 12 ♘c4 ♕d8

If 12...♕c7 the white attack is relentless after 13 ♗c6 ♗b7 (13...♖b8 14 ♕f3, intending ♗f4, gives White the advantage) 14 ♘b5 ♕b8 15 ♕e2 and the threat of ♘d6+ is good news for White.

13 ♘xa4 ♗b7 14 ♕e2!

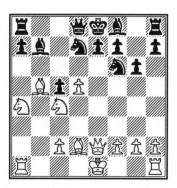

The big idea is 15 ♘d6 checkmate.

14...♕b8 15 ♖b1 ♗g7

What else? 15...♔d8 looks a desperate way to try and escape the pins and indeed 16 ♗a5+ ♔c8 17 ♕e3 is crushing for White.

16 ♗xd7+ ♘xd7 17 ♖xb7! 1-0

Perhaps Black's best chance lies in moving the knight away from the attentions of the dark-squared bishop.

Burmakin-Avrukh

Ubeda 2001

1 d4 ♘f6 2 ♘f3 c5 3 d5 b5 4 ♗g5 ♘e4 5 ♗h4

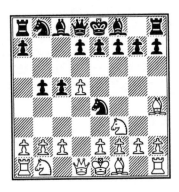

This bishop retreat has Kasparov's seal of approval.

5...♗b7

The attack on the d5 pawn has rapidly established itself as the main line. Kasparov-Miles, 3rd match game, Basel 1986, saw 5...♕a5+ but it has not really caught on. That game went 6 ♘bd2 ♗b7 7 a4 ♗xd5 (7...♘xd2 has been touted as an improvement but Ikonnikov-Szieberth, Budapest 1998 is not a great advert for Black's chances after 8 ♘xd2 ♗xd5 9 axb5 ♕c7 10 e3 g6 11 ♘c4 ♗b7 12 ♗e2 d6 13 ♘a5! ♗g7 14 ♗f3 ♗xf3 15 ♕xf3 0-0 16 ♕xa8 ♗xb2 17 0-0 1-0) 8 axb5 ♕c7 (or 8...♕b4 9 c4 ♗b7 10 ♕c2 ♘xd2 11 ♘xd2 g5 12 ♖a4 winning, Yakovich-Scetinin, Leeuwarden 1995) 9 ♖a4 ♕b7 10 c4 ♘xd2 and now, instead of 11 cxd5 ♘xf1 12 ♕d3 d6 13 e4! ♘d7 14 ♕xf1 with an edge, in the actual game Kasparov suggests White is better after 11 ♕xd2 ♗e4 12 e3! d6 13 ♗d3 ♗xf3 14 gxf3 ♕xf3 15 ♖g1 intending to exploit the bishop pair by ♗f1-g2.

6 a4!

White seeks to undermine the queenside pawns which is a policy already examined in the main game Soln-Velicković. The direct approach with 6 ♕d3!? is premature as White found to his cost in Lodhi-Ghaem Maghami, Istanbul Olympiad 2000. That game went 6...f5 7 ♘c3?! (if 7 ♕xb5 then 7...♗xd5 wins back the pawn although 7 ♘bd2 is a safer choice) 7...c4 8 ♕d4 ♕a5 9 e3 (9 ♘d2 has been suggested as an improvement but 9...♘xd2

10 ♕xd2 b4 11 ♘d1 ♗xd5 leaves Black simply a pawn up) 9...e6 10 dxe6 dxe6 11 0-0-0 (Black must watch out for checkmate on d8) 11...♗d5! 12 ♘xe4 (White is already in trouble because 12 ♘xd5 is well met by 12...♘c6 with advantage to Black) 12...fxe4 13 ♘e5 ♕xa2 14 ♘xc4 (14 ♕xe4 could be played with a smile because 14...♗xe4?? allows 15 ♖d8 mate but, on the other hand, 14...♕a1+ 15 ♔d2 ♕a5+ *does* enable Black to capture the white queen) 14...♘c6 0-1.

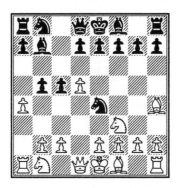

6...a6!?

Black logically supports the b-pawn—which is the favoured response in all the old opening books.

Others:

a) 6...bxa4?! allows White to activate the queen's rook to his advantage: 7 ♖xa4 f5 8 g4 (an aggressive reply which is motivated by the fact that Black cannot support the pawn with ...e7-e6 because it is pinned by the bishop on h4) 8...fxg4 (or 8...g6 9 gxf5 gxf5 10 ♗h3 with good chances for White) 9 ♖xe4 gxf3 10 exf3 ♘a6 11 ♘a3 ♘c7 12 c4 d6 13 ♗h3 (White's superiority is based principally on his space advantage which gives him freedom to develop and manoeuvre his pieces) 13...♗c8 14 ♗xc8 ♕xc8 15 0-0 g5 (a tricky idea but in the circumstances understandable because White has strong pressure against e7) 16 ♗xg5 ♖g8 17 ♖g4 ♕f5 18 ♗xe7! ♖g6 19 ♗h4 ♔f7 20 ♘c2 ♖e8 21 ♘e3 ♕h5 22 ♗g3 ♗h6 23 ♕d3 1-0 Yakovich-Rat, Stockholm 2002.

b) 6...b4?! 7 ♕d3! (the difference compared to other lines is that ...c5-c4 is no longer a worry since the supporting b-pawn has advanced to b4) 7...f5 8 ♘bd2 ♗a6 9 ♕b3 ♘xd2 10 ♘xd2 ♕c7 (10...g6 is well met by 11 e4! when 11...♗xf1 12 ♔xf1 ♗h6 13 ♘c4 g5 {13...fxe4 14 ♘d6+! ♔f8 15 ♘xe4 is excellent for White} 14 ♕f3! 0-0 15 ♕h5 gxh4 16 ♕xh6 gives White a tremendous attack) 11 e4 ♗xf1 12 ♔xf1 f4 13 ♘c4 (the white knight is well placed on c4 which helps to emphasize the problem of Black's retarded development) 13...e5 14 ♕h3 ♗d6 15 ♕f5! (White stops Black from castling kingside) 15...a5 16 g3 fxg3 17 hxg3 ♖a6 18 ♗g5 h6

19 ♕g6+ ♔f8 20 ♖h5 ♔g8 21 ♕e8+ ♗f8 22 ♘xe5 ♔h7 23 ♗f4 ♕b6 24 ♕f7 ♕b7 25 ♗xh6 1-0 Summerscale-Mannion, British Team Championship (4NCL) 2001.

c) 6...♕a5+ is perhaps the best defence:

c1) 7 ♘bd2 ♗xd5 8 axb5 ♕c7 9 ♖a4 ♘xd2 10 ♕xd2 ♕b7 11 c4 ♗e4 12 e3 d6 13 ♗d3 ♘d7 14 ♕c2 ♗xd3 15 ♕xd3 g6 16 0-0 ♗g7 17 b3 ♘b6 18 ♖a6 ½-½ Gormally-Repkova, Wroxham 2002.

c2) 7 c3 e6 (7...b4 8 c4!) 8 dxe6 fxe6 9 ♘bd2 b4 10 c4! maintains White's slight edge.

7 ♕d3!

Normally White resists the temptation to move the queen early in the opening but the special circumstances of the position demand an active reply. The point is that the queen simultaneously attacks the pawn on b5 and the knight on e4. Instead previous games have focussed on 7 c3 and 7 e3 but after 7...♕b6 White still has to prove an advantage.

7...♕a5+ 8 c3 f5

Black wants to support his knight but the pawn on f5 is fragile. Perhaps 8...♘f6 is the right way to admit that the opening has gone wrong although after 8...♘f6 9 e4 e6 10 ♗xf6 gxf6 11 ♘bd2 c4 12 ♕d4 ♗e7 13 b3 is simply good for White.

9 ♘bd2 e6

9...c4, to knock the queen off its perch, is worth a go when 10 ♕d4 e6 11 ♘xe4 fxe4 12 ♕xe4 ♗xd5 13 ♕f4 ♗xf3! (otherwise 14 ♘e5 is a killer) 14 ♕xf3 ♘c6 15 g3 offers White the better prospects because it is easier for his king to dash to safety by castling kingside.

10 ♘xe4 fxe4 11 ♕xe4 ♗xd5 12 ♕f4 ♘c6 13 e4!

Burmakin wants to use his king's knight for a forthcoming attack so he deflects the bishop away from the centre and thereby allows Black no chance to exchange pieces on f3.

13...♗b3 14 ♗e2!

The fate of a mere pawn is insignificant when compared to White's need to accelerate his development in the name of attack.

14...bxa4

Black has to do something to cope with White's threat of short castling, to co-ordinate the rooks, and then axb5. If 14...b4 then 15 c4 makes Black's light-squared bishop look rather silly. For instance: 15...♗c2 16 0-0 b3 17 ♘g5 ♘d8 18 ♗h5+ g6 19 ♕e5! ♖g8 20 ♘xh7 and Black is busted.

15 0-0 ♗e7

Avrukh has to do something because his king is stuck in the centre and so he endeavours to mobilise his kingside pieces.

16 ♗xe7 ♘xe7?!

I doubt if there would be many volunteers ready to try 16...♔xe7 but it is necessary.

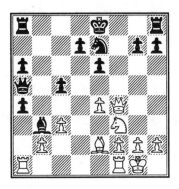

17 ♘e5

A clearer course to victory lies in 17 ♘g5! ♖f8 18 ♕e5 when the black kingside pawns are vulnerable. The game concluded **17...♖f8 18 ♕g3 g6 19 ♗c4 ♕c7 20 ♗xb3 axb3 21 ♖fd1 d5 22 c4 a5** (the weakness of Black's queenside pawns is a worry after 22...d4 23 ♘d3 ♕xg3 24 hxg3) **23 f4 0-0-0** (or 23...d4 24 ♕xb3 ♖xf4 25 ♕b5+ ♔f8 26 ♘d7+ ♔g8 27 ♘xc5 winning) **24 ♕g4! ♔b7** (24...dxe4 does not inspire confidence after 25 ♕xe6+ ♔b7 26 ♘f7 with a clear advantage) **25 ♕xe6 ♖d6 26 ♕g4 h5** (26...dxe4 27 ♖xd6 ♕xd6 28 ♖d1 or 26...d4 27 ♖d3 wins) **27 ♕f3 g5** (Black tries to complicate matters in view of 27...dxc4 28 ♘xc4 ♖xd1+ 29 ♕xd1 winning) **28 ♕xb3+ ♖b6 29 ♕a3 gxf4 30 ♕xa5 ♖b8 31 ♘d3 ♘c6 32 ♘xc5+ ♔c8 33 ♕c3 ♘e5 34 ♖xd5 1-0**

SUMMARY

The key to White's strategy is 4 ♗g5, which threatens to exchange a knight on f6 and double the f-pawns. In the game **Izeta Txabarri-Bellon Lopez** Black sees this as no problem and tries 4...♗b7 to attack the d5 pawn. In a closed position White's pieces flourish behind a wall of pawns where his space advantage makes it easier to manoeuvre. A queen sortie with 4...♕b6 is examined in **Soln-Velickovic**. Black wants to keep his pawn structure intact by recapturing on f6 with the queen but is lured into a complicated line by White. 4...♘e4 is the subject in **Burmakin-Avrukh** with White responding aggressively by striving to undermine the queenside pawns.

THE QUEEN'S INDIAN FORMATIONS

The Queen's Indian is a popular defence usually employed by Nimzo-Indian players when faced with ♘f3 rather than 3 ♘c3. Black plays a queenside fianchetto and fights for control of the e4 square.

HISTORY OF THE QUEEN'S INDIAN

This opening normally occurs after the sequence 1 d4 ♘f6 2 c4 e6 3 ♘f3 b6. Aron Nimzowitsch (1886-1935) popularised the continuation during the 'Hypermodern' revolution of the 1920s. It allows rapid development and active play against the white centre and has found its way into the repertoires of players of every level, even including such chess stars as Adams, Anand, and Karpov.

IDEAS BEHIND THE OPENING

Against the London System a Queen's Indian player is likely to play his familiar formation. However, with no pawn on c4, Black enters relatively unexplored territory. After developing his pieces White usually contemplates taking over the centre with e3-e4. The American grandmaster Larry Christiansen has used the system with success on numerous occasions.

HOW TO BEAT THE QUEEN'S INDIAN

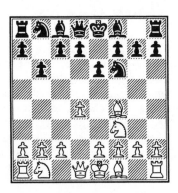

As usual White adopts the London System to combat Black's formation. The option of c2-c4 is usually held in reserve during the opening and more interest is directed at the possibility of a later e3-e4 to take over the centre. The difference compared to normal Queen's Indian lines is that ...c7-c5 can be rebuffed with c2-c3 supporting the d-pawn.

Christiansen-D.Gurevich
Philadelphia 1988

1 d4 ♘f6 2 ♘f3 e6 3 ♗f4 b6 4 e3 c5 5 ♗d3

Anyone who plays the London System will once again find the opening strategy familiar. White is able to speedily develop his pieces without worrying about any tricks or traps.

5...♗b7 6 c3 ♗e7

The tempting 6...♘h5?!, to exchange the dark-squared bishop, is inaccurate, e.g. 7 ♗g5 f6 8 ♗h4 g5? 9 ♘xg5 and White wins.

7 h3

Now that the bishop on e7 is covering the g5 square White needs to be wary of allowing his influential bishop to be exchanged by ...♘h5, so he creates an escape square. In R.Zimmerman-Adams, Kilkenny 1997, White wavered with 7 ♘bd2 allowing Black to achieve equality by 7...♘h5. There followed 8 ♗g3 g6 (a little bit unusual but it can be played with confidence if you are one of the top players in the world!) 9 0-0 (9 ♗e5 is met by 9...0-0 and it is only Black who has boosted his development) 9...0-0 10 e4 d6 11 ♖e1 cxd4 12 cxd4 ♘c6 13 ♖c1 a6 14 a3 ♘xg3 15 hxg3 ♗f6 with equal chances.

7...0-0 8 0-0 d6 9 ♕e2

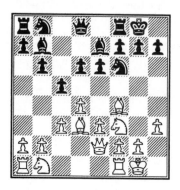

The queen prepares the advance e2-e4. This continuation tends to make for a sophisticated battle where White hopes to create tactical opportunities by virtue of the greater flexibility of his position. 9 0-0 is discussed in the next illustrative game. 9 ♘bd2 is the other major alternative where the positions are worth investigating because of their similarity to the main game if Black improves by exchanging on d4. For example:

a) 9...♘bd7 10 ♕e2 cxd4 (otherwise White advances the e-pawn along the lines of the main game) 11 cxd4 (11 exd4!?) 11...♘d5 12 ♗g3 ♘b4 13 ♗b5 a6 14 ♗a4 b5 15 ♗b3 ♘b6 16 e4 (at last White has found time to advance the e-pawn but now Black's pieces are actively placed on the queenside) 16...♖c8 17 ♖ac1 ♕d7 18 a3 ♖xc1 19 ♖xc1 ♘c6 20 ♗c2 ♘a5 21 ♗d3 ♖c8 22 ♕e1 ♘ac4 with equal chances in Dzindzichashvili-Rohde, New York 1994.

b) 9...♘c6 10 a3 (White wants to play e3-e4 but, after an exchange of pawns on d4, is concerned that Black's queen's knight will come to the b4 square and exchange his light-squared bishop) 10...♖c8 11 ♗h2 ♕c7 12 e4 e5 (otherwise White is continually threatening e4-e5 to open up the diagonal of his bishop to h7) 13 dxc5 dxc5 14 ♘c4 gave White play against the e5 pawn, Wallace-Weeks, Sydney 1999.

c) 9...cxd4 10 exd4 ♘bd7 11 ♖e1 (perhaps 11 ♕e2!? can be considered) 11...a6 12 a4 (simply to prevent Black gaining space with ...b6-b5) 12...♖e8 13 ♕e2 ♕c8 14 ♗h2 ♗c6 15 ♘g5 offers White the slightly better chances due to his space advantage Rozić-Simon, Balatonlelle 2002.

9...♘bd7?!

Black carries on developing but it is a passive response in view of White's threatened expansion in the centre. Therefore 9...cxd4 is preferable or 9...♘c6 when 10 e4?! cxd4 11 cxd4 ♘b4 is fine for Black who can exchange the important light-squared bishop.

10 e4

This advance is not often made in the London System but Black's passive set-up is a signal for White to play energetically.

10...cxd4 11 cxd4 ♖e8 12 ♘c3 ♗f8 13 ♖fd1

In his analysis of the game—upon which these notes are based—Christiansen criticises this move because he believes 13 e5! is a winner. For example: 13...dxe5 14 dxe5 ♘d5 (14...♗xf3 15 ♕xf3 ♘d5 16 ♗e4 is good for White) 15 ♗xh7+ ♔xh7 16 ♘g5+ ♔g6 17 ♕d3+ f5 18 exf6+ ♔xf6 19 ♘ce4+ winning. However, I think 14...♘c5! allows Black to hang on thanks to various tactical tricks, e.g. 15 ♗c4 (or 15 ♗b5 ♘fd7 16 b4 a6!) 15...♕c7 16 ♘b5 ♕b8 17 ♖fd1 ♘d5 and White still has some way to go before proving a decisive advantage.

13...g6 14 ♖ac1

Another piece is brought into the action. Now the threat is ♘b5—to target the d6 pawn and introduce the possibility of ♘c7 forking the rooks.

14...a6 15 a4!? ♖a7?!

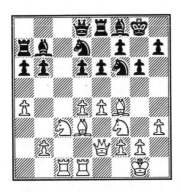

Black is trying to be clever by clearing the a8 square for the queen in order to exert more pressure on the h1-a8 diagonal. It is certainly a valid idea in some positions but this is not one of them because there are enough pawn breaks available to White to exploit the absence of the black queen from the action. 15...e5!? is a better bet although White remains on top after 16 dxe5 dxe5 17 ♗g5 intending ♗c4.

16 e5 dxe5 17 dxe5 ♘d5

17...♘h5 18 ♗h2 ♗h6 19 ♖c2 ♖a8 20 ♗e4 is good for White because of the pin on the d-file.

18 ♘xd5 exd5

If 18...♗xd5 then White should avoid the pawn grab 19 ♗xa6 when 19...♗xf3 20 gxf3 ♕h4! gives Black chances of survival. Instead, 19 ♗c4 ♘c5 20 b4 ♘xa4 21 ♕a2 is better for White.

19 ♕d2 d4?!

19...♘c5! 20 ♗c2 ♘e6 21 ♗e3 a5 22 ♗b3 still favours White.

20 e6!

A quality move that allows the white knight to take on d4 and gain crucial time. Instead the tame 20 ♘xd4 is well met by 20...♘xe5 with equality.

20...♖xe6

If 20...fxe6? then 21 ♘xd4 e5 (21...♘c5 22 ♗c4!) 22 ♗c4+ ♔h8 23 ♘e6 wins.

21 ♘xd4 ♖e8

22 ♘b5!

A tremendous sacrifice which allows White to make maximum use of the pin on the d-file. Such an idea is possible due to the misplaced black pieces. Instead Christiansen presents the pretty line 22 ♖c7 ♘e5! 23 ♖xb7 ♖xb7 24 ♗xe5 ♖xe5 25 ♘c6 ♕e8 26 ♘xe5 ♕xe5 27 ♗xa6 with advantage to White. However, the whole sequence is thwarted by 22...♗h6! to distract the defender of the rook on c7.

22...axb5 23 ♗xb5 ♗c8?!

In the face of heavy odds Black tries to defend the knight. Other moves:

a) 23...♗a8 24 ♗xd7 ♖e7 25 ♖c8 ♕xd7 26 ♕xd7 ♖exd7 27 ♖xd7 ♖xd7 28 ♗h6 wins.

b) 23...♗a6! (this is the best choice available) 24 ♗xd7 (24 ♗xa6 ♖xa6 25 ♕xd7 ♕xd7 26 ♖xd7 ♖xa4 is equal) 24...♖e2 25 ♕d5 ♗c5 26 ♗g5 ♕f8 (or 26...♗xf2+ 27 ♔h1 ♕b8 28 ♗g4 ♖xb2?? 29 ♖c8+ ♗xc8 30 ♕d8+ ♔g7 31 ♗f6+ ♔h6 32 ♕f8 mate) 27 ♗h4 when White is still the favourite.

24 ♖xc8 ♕xc8 25 ♗xd7 ♖xd7 26 ♕xd7 ♕xd7

If 26...♖e1+ then 27 ♔h2 side-steps any trap.

27 ℤxd7 ℤe4 28 ♗e3 ♗c5?

This obvious-looking move makes White's task easier. Instead 28...ℤxa4 29 ℤd8 ♔g7 30 ♗d4+ ♔h6 31 ♗xb6 still leaves White some work to do before converting the extra pawn into victory.

29 ♗h6

The threat of mate prompts Gurevich to reduce his rook to a role where it must temporarily defend the back rank. It is this factor that allows White to continually improve his position. The game concluded:

29...ℤe8 30 ♔f1 ♗f8 31 ♗e3 ♗c5 32 ♗d2! ℤe4 33 ♗c3 f6 34 b3 ♗e7 35 ♗d4 ♗b4 36 ♗e3 ♗c5 37 ♗d2 ♗e7 38 ℤb7 ℤe6 39 ♗e3 ♗c5 40 ♗xc5! bxc5 41 ℤc7 ℤb6 42 a5 ℤb8 43 a6 1-0

It is also possible for Black to carry on developing and defer any advance of the queen's pawn. This will keep White guessing about Black's intended pawn formation.

Dudas-Allen
Budapest 1997

1 d4 ♘f6 2 ♘f3 e6 3 ♗f4 c5

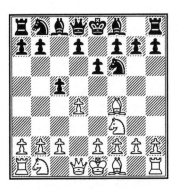

This is a common response but White can still stick to his standard set-up.

4 e3 b6 5 c3 ♗b7 6 ♘bd2 ♗e7 7 h3 ♘c6 8 ♗d3 0-0 9 0-0

This whole line is similar to the previous game except Black has delayed moving the queen's pawn. It is just another example of how White can emerge from the opening with a decent position by following the basic plan and without worrying about having to learn lots of theory. Also possible is 9 ♕e2 when the game Kovacević-Dutoit, Mendrisio 1989, continued 9...d6 10 0-0 h6 11 a4 (White wants to play ♘c4 but is concerned about a speedy ...b6-b5) 11...♖e8 12 ♖fd1 ♗f8 13 ♘c4 d5 14 ♘ce5 gave White a comfortable game due to the imposing knight on e5.

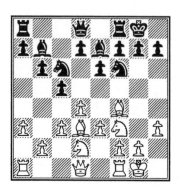

9...♖c8

A move that has the seal of approval of David Bronstein who once drew a match for the world championship. The intention is to activate the rook on the c-file after exchanging pawns in the centre. Other moves are:

a) 9...cxd4 10 exd4

a1) 10...a6 11 a4 ♘d5 12 ♗h2 f5 (Black controls the e4 square although White will now have the option of ♘d2-c4-e5) 13 ♖e1 ♖f6 14 ♗f1 (the bishop retreats to enable White to drive the knight away from its central position) 14...♔h8 15 c4 ♘db4 16 ♘b3 ♘a5 17 ♘xa5 bxa5 (the doubled a-pawns are a long-term worry) 18 ♖c1 ♖f8 19 ♘e5 ♗f6 20 ♕h5 gave White the better chances in Christiansen-Kindermann, German Team Ch 1989.

a2) 10...d6 11 ♖e1 ♖e8 12 ♘c4 ♘d5 13 ♗g3 g6 (or 13...b5 14 ♘e3 ♘xe3 15 ♖xe3 a6 16 d5! exd5 17 ♗c2, intending ♕d3, offers good practical chances) 14 a4 a6 15 h4!? (a great idea to soften up the black kingside—if the pawn advance is blocked by ...h5 then White will have a useful outpost on g5) 15...♘a5 16 ♘cd2 ♘f6 17 b4 (gaining space) 17...♘c6 18 ♘g5 ♘h5 19 ♗h2 e5 20 d5 ♘b8 21 ♕f3 ♖f8 22 ♘xh7! with a winning attack, Christiansen-Peter, Bad Mergentheim 1988.

b) 9...d5 (in this line Black is usually keen to control the e5 square to stop White planting a knight there) 10 a4 ♖e8 11 ♘e5 ♗d6 12 ♘df3 h6 13 ♘xc6 ♗xc6 14 ♗xd6 ♕xd6 15 ♘e5 c4 16 ♗c2 a6 17 f4 (with the centre closed White can advance the pawns in front of his king without fear of infiltration by the black pieces) 17...♖e7 18 g4 with attacking prospects, Alvarez Fernandez-Cascudo Pueyo, Aviles 2001.

10 a3!?

The idea is to stop the black knight coming to b4 after the exchange of pawns in the centre.

Also possible is 10 ♕e2 d6 (or 10...cxd4 11 exd4 d6 12 ♖fe1 ♖c7 13 a4 ♕c8 14 ♘c4 ♖d8 15 a5 with the better chances, Wesseln-Zude, Dudweiler 1996) 11 ♖ad1 (if 11 e4?! then 11...cxd4 12 cxd4 ♘b4 allows Black to equalise by exchanging pieces on d3 because 13 ♗b1? loses disastrously to 13...♗a6) 11...♖c7 12 ♗h2 ♕a8 13 a3 cxd4 14 exd4 ♘b8 15 ♖fe1 with roughly equal chances, Franklin-Sowray, British Team Ch (4NCL) 2000.

10...d6

Black can also ease the tension in the centre by 10...cxd4 when White can keep his centre pawns intact with 11 cxd4 because the b4 square is covered. Jaluvka-Yeremenko, ICCF e-mail Ch 1999, went 11...d6 12 ♕e2 ♕d7 13 e4 (White takes the opportunity to create a pawn centre) 13...♖fd8 14 ♗b5 d5 15 e5 ♘h5 16 ♗e3 giving White the better chances because the knight on h5 is misplaced. It is worth mentioning that 10...d5 concedes the e5 square so 11 ♘e5 is a good reaction although even 11 b4 has been tested in a bid to block the queenside before launching a kingside attack.

11 ♗h2 ♖e8 12 ♕e2 ♗f8 13 ♖ac1 e5

White wants to break out of his restricted position by this advance which now threatens ...e5-e4 forking the white pieces.

14 dxe5 dxe5 15 ♗f5 ♖a8 16 ♖fd1

Placing a rook on the d-file may be obvious but here it also serves the purpose of persuading Black to move his queen and go on the defensive.

16...♕e7 17 ♘e4 ♖ed8?!

Black needs to defend against the threat of ♘d6 but 17...♖ad8 should be considered because then White's game continuation would not be so effective as there is still a rook defending the e5 pawn. Nevertheless 18 ♗g3, intending ♗h4, would still preserve White's initiative.

18 ♘xf6+ ♕xf6 19 ♗e4

The direct threat is 19 ♘xe5 to exploit the pinned queen's knight.

19...♗d6 20 ♗g3

Dudas relentlessly continues to apply pressure—now Black has to deal with the prospect of ♗h4.

20...♕e6?

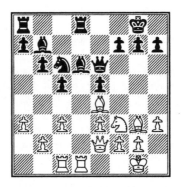

20...♕e7 is necessary, intending to meet 21 ♗h4 with 21...f6.

21 ♗xh7+!

This nice little tactic gives White a clear advantage. The bishop is taboo because of the resulting fork of king and queen after 21...♔xh7 22 ♘g5+.

21...♔f8 22 ♗e4 ♗c7 23 ♘g5

Now that the black king has been stripped of its defensive pawn barrier it makes sense to keep attacking.

23...♕h6 24 h4 g6 25 ♕f3! 1-0

An early exchange of pawns on d4 is popular nowadays. White should keep out of trouble by developing his pieces in similar fashion to the previous main games.

Eliet-Salaun
Bogny sur Meuse 2002

1 d4 ♘f6 2 ♘f3 e6 3 ♗f4 b6 4 ♘bd2 ♗b7 5 e3 ♗e7 6 ♗d3 c5 7 c3 cxd4 8 exd4 0-0

If 8...d6 then 9 ♕e2 ♘bd7 10 0-0 0-0 11 ♖fe1 (White carries on centralising his pieces until Black reveals his intentions) 11...♖e8 12 ♘g5 ♗f8 13 ♗c4 ♘d5? (13...h6? 14 ♘xf7! ♔xf7 15 ♗xe6+ ♖xe6 16 ♕xe6+ ♔g6 17 ♗xd6 is better for White) 14 ♕h5 1-0 Linden-Haapasalo, Helsinki 1999.

9 ♕e2

Accelerating the attack by 9 h4 is an adventurous idea examined in Blatny-Chuchelov, German Team Ch 1993. That game went 9...d6 10 ♕e2 a6 11 ♘g5 ♘bd7 12 0-0-0 ♖e8 13 ♖h3 b5 14 ♘df3 ♘f8 15 ♕c2 ♕a5 when Black has enough pieces to fend off the onslaught and is ready to create counterplay on the queenside.

9 h3 gives the bishop another escape square. For example: 9...d6 10 ♕e2 ♖e8 11 0-0 ♘bd7 12 ♘c4 ♘f8 13 ♖fe1 ♘g6 14 ♗h2 ♘d5 15 ♕d2 with a level position, Van de Mortel-Pliester, Leeuwarden 1993.

9...♘c6

Or 9...♘h5 to exchange off the dark-squared bishop when Salman-Reshevsky, Philadelphia 1987, continued 10 ♗e3 (10 ♗g3 ♘xg3 11 hxg3 h6 12 0-0-0!? gives White attacking chances due to the semi-open h-file) 10...♘f6 11 0-0-0 ♘d5 12 h4 with sharp play.

10 h3 a6 11 a4 b5!?

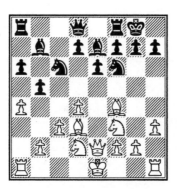

A surprising pawn advance because it seemed that White had stopped it with his previous move. On closer inspection, however, it is the fact that White has not yet castled which makes all the difference. Thus the attempt to win the b-pawn rebounds after 12 axb5 axb5 13 ♖xa8 ♕xa8 14 ♗xb5? ♕a1+ 15 ♕d1 ♕xb2 16 ♗d3 ♕xc3 and the white position collapses

12 0-0

A sensible response which reinforces the pressure on b5.

12...bxa4?!

Black saddles himself with a long-term problem in the form of the isolated a-pawn. 12...b4 seems to be a good choice when White has to rely on his space advantage for an edge.

13 ♖xa4 ♘d5 14 ♗h2 a5 15 ♖e1

Eliet gets another piece into the action although doubling rooks by 15 ♖fa1—and intending ♘c4—also looks useful.

15...♘b6 16 ♖aa1 a4 17 ♘e4 ♘a5?!

Black has pushed the a-pawn to facilitate this knight manoeuvre but it would be more prudent to play 17...d6 to stop the white knight invading on c5.

18 ♘c5 ♗d5

18...♗xc5? 19 dxc5 ♘d5 20 ♖xa4 just leaves White a pawn up.

19 ♘d2 ♘b7 20 c4

White has the initiative because Black is in a tangle over the defence of the a-pawn.

20...♗c6 21 ♘xb7 ♗xb7 22 c5 ♘d5 23 ♘c4

White has control over the d6 square, right in the heart of Black's position, and must be better.

23...♗f6 24 ♕g4

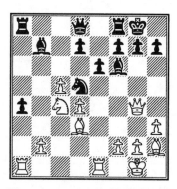

The white queen finds a superior position from where it can bolster the attack.

24...g6

White also retains a firm grip after 24...♗c6 25 ♗d6 ♖e8 26 ♘e5.

25 ♗d6 h5

25...♖e8 26 ♗e5 ♗e7 27 ♖a3, intending to double rooks, is another example of White's control of the game.

26 ♕d1 ♗xd4!?

Salun realises that his position is bleak and so tries to conjure up some counterplay rather than wait to be slowly crushed.

27 ♗xf8 ♕h4 28 ♕f3 ♖xf8 29 ♖e4

White is on top and with correct play should triumph—but he eventually goes astray. The game concluded:

29...♕f6 30 ♕xf6 ♗xf6 31 ♖xa4 ♗c6 32 ♖a3 ♖b8 33 ♘b6?

33 ♖e1 is a clear improvement as 33...♗xb2 loses to 34 ♖b1.

33...♗e7 34 ♘xd5 ♗xd5 35 ♖e2 ♗xc5 36 ♖a5 ♗d4 37 ♖b5 ♖a8 38 ♖e1 ♔g7 39 ♖d1 ♗c6 40 ♖b3 ♗e5 41 ♖b1 g5 42 ♖a3 ♖b8 43 b4 ♗d5 44 ♖a7 g4 45 h4 g3 46 ♖xd7 gxf2+ 47 ♔f1 ♗a2 48 ♖c1 ♖xb4 49 ♔xf2 ♖xh4 50 ♗e2 ♖f4+ 51 ♔e3 ♗d5 52 ♗xh5 ♖f5 53 ♖h1 ♗xg2 ½-½

SUMMARY

Christiansen-D.Gurevich is a demonstration that the London System has adherents at the highest level. Here White mobilises his forces quickly for the middlegame battle. It is worth noting that Black's reluctance to play ...d5 in some cases allows e3-e4 to exert greater control over the centre. Another example of how familiarity with our recommended set-up can reap dividends is clear from the game **Dudas-Allen**. Although White doesn't appear to do anything special, he slowly increases his space advantage while Black is left struggling to find any targets. Finally, **Eliet-Salaun** is 'the one that got away'. Black eases the tension in the centre by exchanging pawns and White is able to simply carry on developing until he achieves a winning position—but he fails to convert it.

THE GRÜNFELD
FORMATIONS

The Grünfeld formation is a popular system against the London System because it can arise after 1 d4 d5 or 1 d4 ♘f6 and involves a kingside fianchetto. This flexibility makes it important for White to be aware of the various plans available.

HISTORY OF THE GRÜNFELD

The Grünfeld normally occurs after 1 d4 ♘f6 2 c4 g6 3 ♘c3 d5 and was introduced to a wider audience by the Viennese grandmaster Ernst Grünfeld (1893-1962) who played it extensively in the 1920s. Over recent years it has grown in popularity and is favoured by Garry Kasparov.

IDEAS BEHIND THE OPENING

Anyone who plays the Grünfeld will seek to fianchetto on the kingside and stake a claim in the centre by playing an early ...d7-d5. In the main line Grünfeld, novelties are routinely being introduced after move 20—which is fine if you have a good memory and a lot of spare time! It is a different story against the London System where the solid formation offers Black a minimal amount of tricks and traps.

HOW TO BEAT THE GRÜNFELD

The opening revolves around playing ...d7-d5 to challenge the white centre and the pawn on c4. However, the move-order of the London System makes the labyrinth of variations in the Grünfeld redundant. But it is still possible for Black to employ his basic formation despite there being no white pawn on c4 and the following diagram shows the resulting position which is analysed in the present chapter.

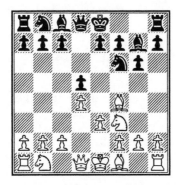

So the key to success against a Grünfeld formation is to uphold the good habits of the London, such as rapid development, a solid pawn structure and the possibility of a kingside attack. It is important to note that the position can occur via 1 d4 d5 ♘f3 ♘f6 3 ♗f4 g6 4 e3 ♗g7 or 1 d4 ♘f6 2 ♘f3 g6 3 ♗f4 ♗g7 4 e3 d5.

Kharlov-Hillarp Persson
Skelleftea 1999

1 d4 ♘f6 2 ♘f3 g6 3 ♗f4 ♗g7 4 e3 d5

This is the typical Grünfeld structure. Of course, the pawn on d5 stops White from creating a big pawn centre but the absence of a pawn on c4 is relatively unusual and will not make a Grünfeld expert happy. For conformity I have used the same move-orders in all the games although in this example the game originally began 1 d4 d5 2 ♘f3 ♘f6 3 ♗f4 g6 4 e3 ♗g7 transposing to the text.

5 ♗d3

White gets on with the job of developing. The long-term plan is to advance the e-pawn.

5...c5

Black tries to undermine the central pawn structure.

Other moves are:

a) 5...♗g4 (the pin on the knight is a popular reply although fairly harmless) 6 ♘bd2 (a simple solution to protect the pinned knight and with the intention of following up with h2-h3) 6...♘bd7 7 0-0 0-0 8 h3 ♗xf3 9 ♘xf3 c5 10 c3 c4 11 ♗c2 ♘b6 12 ♖e1 (12 ♘d2, intending to play e3-e4, looks reasonable so that after exchanges on e4 White can take back with the knight and retain his bishop pair) 12...♖e8 13 e4 ♘xe4 14 ♗xe4 dxe4 15 ♖xe4 gave White a slight edge in Kuijper-Schoenmakers, Soest 2001.

b) 5...0-0 6 0-0 ♗f5!? (Black wants to contest White's control of the e4 square whereas 6...c5 7 c3 would transpose to the main game) 7 ♗xf5 gxf5 8 c4 dxc4 9 ♕c2 is fine for White, Agh-Juracsik, Budapest 2002.

6 c3 ♘c6 7 ♘bd2 0-0

7...♘h5 is possible, seeking to exchange the dark-squared bishop, but then 8 ♗g5 h6 9 ♗h4 g5 10 ♗g3 ♘xg3 11 hxg3 is better for White because the semi-open h-file can be used by the king's rook to attack Black's weakened kingside.

8 h3

A familiar idea in this system to give the bishop an escape square. This is necessary because when White castles kingside there will no longer be a rook on h1 to benefit from the open h-file if Black exchanges knight for bishop on g3.

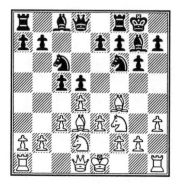

8...♘d7

Black could release the central tension with 8...c4 when the game Conquest-Lewis, British Ch 1985, continued 9 ♗c2 ♗f5!? (otherwise White plays e3-e4 with an edge) 10 ♗xf5 gxf5 11 g4! (a typical attacking idea by White to weaken Black's hold on the e4 square) 11...♕d7 (if 11...fxg4 12 hxg4 ♘xg4 13 ♕c2 f5 14 ♘g5 and the twin threats of ♘e6 and ♘xh7 give White the upper hand) 12 ♕c2 ♘e4 13 ♖g1 (White is renowned for his on-slaughts so it is no surprise that he adds the rook to the g-file in preparation of a direct attack) 13...f6 14 gxf5 ♕xf5 15 0-0-0 (the king is sheltered and more importantly the queen's rook is now available for offensive duties) 15...♔f7 16 ♖g4 ♖g8 17 ♖dg1 ♗h8 18 ♘h4! (the black queen is over-worked and the black defences collapse) 18...♖xg4 19 hxg4 ♕e6 20 f3 ♘g5 21 ♗xg5 fxg5 22 ♕xh7+ ♗g7 23 ♕h5+ ♔g8 24 ♕xg5 winning.

9 0-0 e5

This is a classic way of countering the London System—Black contests White's dominance of the e5 square.

10 dxe5 ♘dxe5 11 ♗c2

Although Black is active it is not clear how he can make progress and this allows White to utilise his solid foundations to probe for weaknesses.

11...h6 12 ♘xe5 ♘xe5 13 e4!

An excellent move which challenges the d5 pawn and helps White's pieces to flourish.

13...dxe4 14 ♘xe4 b6

If 14...♕xd1 15 ♖axd1 b6 16 ♘d6 the knight on d6 is very strong and after 16...♗e6 17 b3 White has the better chances in the ending.

15 ♘d6!

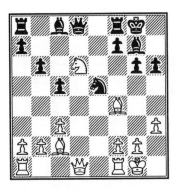

The knight is a dominating figure on d6, promoting tactical tricks and making it very difficult for Black to co-ordinate his rooks on the central files.

15...♕f6

Or 15...♗e6 when the tactics roll after 16 ♖e1 ♘c4 17 ♗e4! ♘xb2 18 ♕e2 with advantage to White.

16 ♗xe5 ♕xe5 17 ♖e1 ♕g5 18 ♗e4 ♖b8 19 ♗d5 ♗xh3

Black wins a pawn and has vague mating threats. However White is well placed to cope with these which is also the case in other lines. For instance:

a) 19...♗d7 20 ♘xf7 ♖xf7 21 ♗xf7+ ♔xf7 22 ♕xd7+.

b) 19...b5 20 ♘xf7 ♖xf7 21 ♖e8+ ♗f8 22 ♗xf7+ ♔xf7 23 ♖xc8 ♖xc8 24 ♕d7+.

c) 19...♕f6 is met by 20 ♖e3, intending ♖f3, when 20...♕xd6 runs into 21 ♗xf7+ winning.

20 ♘xf7 ♖xf7 21 ♗xf7+ ♔h7 22 ♕d5

Karlov stops the threat of mate and at the same time kindly offers Black the choice of entering a lost ending.

22...♗f5 23 ♖ad1 ♗f6 24 ♖e8 ♖xe8 25 ♗xe8 1-0

Another idea is for Black to catch up with development with a queenside fianchetto. But this is a slow system and permits White to play aggressively.

Bawart-Schumi

Austrian Team Championship 1999

1 d4 ♘f6 2 ♘f3 g6 3 ♗f4 ♗g7 4 ♘bd2 d5 5 e3 0-0 6 ♗d3 b6

An understandable reaction by Black who wants to mobilise his queenside pieces. 6...c5 7 c3 transposes to the previous main game.

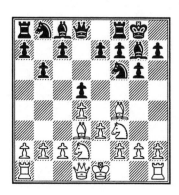

7 ♘e5

7 ♕e2 is another way forward when 7...♝b7 8 h4 demonstrates that the idea of advancing the h-pawn, and using it as a battering ram, is a good attacking device. For example: 8...c5 9 c3 (as usual in this opening the c-pawn cements White's pawn structure) 9...♘bd7 10 0-0-0 ♘e4 11 h5 ♕c8 12 hxg6 fxg6? (12...hxg6 13 ♖h3, intending to double rooks, offers White great chances) 13 ♘xe4 cxd4 (the intended 13...dxe4 backfires after 14 ♝c4+ ♚h8 15 ♖xh7+! ♚xh7 16 ♘g5+ ♚h8 17 ♖h1+ leading to mate) 14 ♘eg5 dxc3 15 ♘e6 and Black can resign with honour, Perez-Palmisano, Buenos Aires 1998. If White wishes to play something more sedate then 7 0-0 is an easy option. Schüssler-Keene, Bochum 1981, continued 7...♝b7 8 ♕e2 c5 9 c3 (a virtually automatic response to Black's advance ...c7-c5) 9 ...♘c6 10 h3 ♘d7 11 ♖ad1 ♖e8 12 ♖fe1 a6 13 ♝c2 e6 when the players decided to pack up the pieces and go home.

7...♝b7 8 h4!?

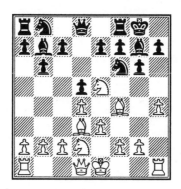

Signalling his intention to attack as soon as possible. The idea of playing a knight to e5 and advancing h2-h4 echos ideas explored in the chapter on 'The Barry Attack'. Alternatively there is the reliable 8 0-0 and also the adventurous 8 ♕f3 when 8...c5 9 h4 ♘c6 10 c3 ♘h5 11 ♘xc6 ♝xc6 12 ♝h2 led to equal chances in Meixner-Ladanyi, Tapolca 1997.

8...♘bd7 9 h5 ♘xe5?!

9...♘xh5 allows White to sacrifice his way to a strong attack by 10 ♖xh5! gxh5 11 ♕xh5 ♘f6 12 ♕h4 c5 (12...♖e8 is a feeble attempt to give the king an escape route and fails to 13 0-0-0 c5 14 ♝h6 ♝xh6 15 ♕xh6 c4 16 ♝xh7+ ♘xh7 17 ♖h1 winning) 13 ♝g5 (the threat is simply to take on f6 to eliminate the defender of h7) 13...c4 14 ♝xf6 cxd3 15 ♝xe7 is better for White. 9...c5 is relatively best but White is still on top thanks to his kingside initiative.

10 dxe5 ♘e4

Once again taking the pawn by 10...♘xh5 leads to ruin: 11 ♖xh5! gxh5 12 ♕xh5 h6 13 ♕f5 ♖e8 14 e6! (a neat trick to block a possible square of escape, otherwise Black is given the chance to play ...e7-e6) 14...fxe6 15 ♕h7+ ♔f8 16 ♗xh6 leads to mate.

11 hxg6 fxg6 12 ♘xe4 dxe4 13 ♗c4+

After just thirteen moves the game is effectively over! The tactics favour White whose opening choice has been a complete success.

13...♖f7

If 13...♔h8 then 14 ♕g4 carries the immediate threat of ♕xg6 and 14...♕e8 is refuted in dramatic fashion by 15 ♖xh7+! ♔xh7 16 ♕h4+ ♗h6 17 ♕xh6 mate.

14 ♗xf7+ ♔xf7 15 ♖xh7

White is the exchange and a pawn up, leaving the final result in no doubt. The game concluded:

15...♔g8 16 ♕xd8+ ♖xd8 17 ♖h1 ♔f7 18 ♖d1 ♖xd1+ 19 ♔xd1 c5 20 ♔c1 ♗d5 21 e6+ ♔xe6 22 ♗b8 ♔d7 23 ♖d1 ♔c6 24 ♗xa7 ♗xa2 25 ♖d8 ♗e5 26 b3 c4 27 ♖c8+ 1-0

SUMMARY

The London System is an irritating opening for the typical Grünfeld player who likes to target the centre because here White just reinforces his pawn structure with c2-c3. This is the case in **Kharlov-Hillarp Persson** where 5...c5 is put to the test. With his pawn centre intact White develops his pieces in the traditional London style and reaches a promising middlegame. **Bawart-Schumi** demonstrates the aggressive h2-h4, similar to an idea in the Barry Attack which is discussed later on in the book. I have also included a calmer approach for those who wish to take the game at a slower pace.

THE KING'S INDIAN DEFENCE

The King's Indian is perhaps the favourite opening of club players against 1 d4. It has been included in the repertoire of many great players, including Bobby Fischer and Garry Kasparov, and remains to this day a reliable opening system with plenty of opportunities for a counterattack.

HISTORY OF THE KING'S INDIAN DEFENCE

The King's Indian Defence is linked to the 1920s Hypermodern school of chess whose followers were content to allow their opponents a big pawn centre in the belief that this could be undermined later in the game. The opening rose to prominence in 1940s when Soviet players such as Bronstein and Boleslavsky championed its cause and by the 1950s it became fashionable throughout the world. It is still held in high esteem and played at all levels.

IDEAS BEHIND THE OPENING

This is the basic King's Indian formation which Black plays against just about everything.

It is clear that a key element is the kingside fianchetto, while the d-pawn is advanced one square to allow the other pieces to develop. In some blocked positional lines Black moves the knight on f6 and then advances his kingside pawns in search of an attack. In fact the great attraction of the King's Indian is precisely this aggressive option—one, however, that is frustrated by the solid, reliable London System.

HOW TO BEAT THE KING'S INDIAN DEFENCE

White should play the London System with confidence and this is the usual position reached after six moves:

Of course there will be no problem remembering all this since it is the basic position used against other openings as well. Here, however, the key factor is how should Black strike back in the centre—with ...c5 or ...e5? In practice the latter is more usual but the centre pawn can easily become a target for White's pieces, especially with the dark-squared bishop and king's knight ideally placed. Perhaps the biggest plus is that Black is stopped from playing in his usual counterattacking style. The resulting solid positions—yet containing scope for tricks and traps—are likely to suit practitioners of the London System.

Payen-Popovych
Philadelphia 1999

1 d4 ♘f6 2 ♘f3 g6 3 ♗f4 ♗g7 4 e3 d6

The bid to exchange the dark-squared bishop by 4...♘h5?! fails to impress after 5 ♗e5 f6 6 g4 when the black kingside is wrecked.

5 h3

White creates an escape square for the bishop. Instead, 5 ♗e2 allows 5...♘h5. For instance: 6 ♗g5 h6 7 ♗h4 g5 8 ♘fd2 ♘f4! (this nuance is awkward to meet) 9 exf4 gxh4 10 c3 c5 11 dxc5 dxc5 12 ♘f3 ♕c7 13 ♘xh4 ♗f6 14 ♘f3 ♕xf4 15 ♘bd2 0-0 gave Black active piece play in Lopushnoy-Bologan, Kazan 1995.

5...0-0 6 ♗e2

This is the classic London System position, which can be played quickly and confidently.

6...♘bd7 7 0-0

7...b6

Black decides to catch up on development with a queenside fianchetto. The main alternatives, 7...c5 and 7...♕e8, are discussed later on in this chapter.

Also possible are:

a) 7...e5?! 8 dxe5 dxe5 (8...♘h5 9 ♗g5 ♕e8 10 ♘c3 ♘xe5 11 ♘d5 is better for White) 9 ♘xe5 ♘xe5 10 ♕xd8 ♖xd8 11 ♗xe5 winning.

b) 7...♖e8 is frowned upon because ...e5 is still not possible due to the pin on the d-file.

c) 7...♘e4 8 ♘bd2 ♘xd2 9 ♕xd2 e5 10 dxe5 (another way to handle the position is 10 ♗h2 ♕e7 11 c4 ♖e8 12 b4 with a level game) 10...dxe5 11 ♗h2 ♕e7 12 e4 ♘c5 13 ♕e3 led to equal chances in Filatov-Kotronias, Philadelphia 2000.

8 ♗h2 ♗b7 9 c3

White keeps faith with the standard London System pawn formation. In this case the intention is to expand on the queen's flank rather than try to storm the black kingside.

9...♘e4 10 ♘bd2 e5

10...♘xd2 11 ♘xd2 e5 12 a4 a6 13 b4 gave White the usual space advantage in Plueg-Ledger, British Team Ch (4NCL) 2001.

11 ♘xe4 ♗xe4 12 a4

Payen finds time to advance his pawns on the queenside. Of course it is not possible to refute the King's Indian but the benefit of the London system is that the opponent is dragged into a positional skirmish when all he wants to do is attack.

12...♕e7 13 a5 ♗xf3?! 14 ♗xf3 e4

Popovych has found a way to advance the kingside pawns but this is not appropriate when there are no reinforcements readily available.

15 ♗e2 ♔h8 16 ♕a4

The queen is ready to infiltrate the weak light-squares in the hunt for material.

16...bxa5

16...f5 is shown to be too slow after 17 ♕c6 ♖ac8 18 axb6 axb6 19 ♖a7 ♘f6 20 ♗a6 when White wins.

17 ♕c6!

A nice idea. White's efforts to target the vulnerable a7 pawn will be a lot easier if he can double rooks on the a-file.

17...♘b6 18 ♖xa5 f5

A last desperate attempt to conjure up active play on the kingside before White plunders the other wing.

19 ♖fa1 ♖f7 20 ♖xa7 ♖af8

21 ♕xb6! 1-0

If Black tries to undermine the pawn centre with ...c7-c5 then White can respond in solid fashion by playing c2-c3 to maintain his pawn structure.

Kudischewitsch-Murey
Tel Aviv 2001

1 d4 ♘f6 2 ♘f3 g6 3 ♗f4 ♗g7 4 e3 d6 5 h3 0-0 6 ♗e2 ♘bd7 7 0-0 c5

Black strikes at the centre.

8 c3

This is a logical reply for anyone who regularly plays the London System and wishes to maintain his pawn structure.

8...b6 9 ♗h2!?

This is an attempt by White to play something a little bit different. The idea is to delay the development of the queen's knight, keeping all options open depending on how Black responds. It has been played successfully by American grandmaster Seirawan so has a good pedigree.

9 ♘bd2 is the main alternative when after 9...♗b7 10 a4 play might continue:

a) 10...a6 (the idea is that if White advances the a-pawn then Black can play ...b6-b5) 11 ♕b3 (11 ♗h2 ♗c6 12 b4 cxb4 13 cxb4 b5 14 a5 ♕c8 15 ♗d3 ♕b7 16 ♕b1 e5 17 e4 ♕a7 18 ♕b3 with a slight plus, Davies-Norman, British Ch 1981) 11...♘e4 12 ♗c4 ♘xd2 13 ♘xd2 e5 14 ♗g3 cxd4 15 exd4 exd4 16 cxd4 ♗xd4 17 ♗xd6 ♘c5 18 ♕g3 ♖e8 19 ♖a2 ♕f6 20 b4 ♘e4 21 ♘xe4 ♖xe4 22 ♖c2 with equal chances, Nguyen Duc Hoa-Bui Duy Toan, Vung Tau 2002.

b) 10...♘d5 11 ♗h2 ♘c7 12 ♕b1!? (a common manoeuvre in this kind of position because from b1 the queen exerts control over the e4 square and assists the advance of the queenside pawns) 12...a6 13 b4 ♘e8 14 ♖c1 ♖c8 15 ♖a2 e5 16 ♖b2 f6 17 bxc5 dxc5 18 ♘c4 when the pressure against the b6 pawn gives White the advantage, Van de Pol-Van der Heijden, Den Bosch 1993.

9...♗b7 10 a4

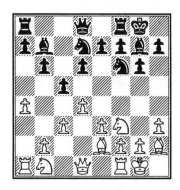

White bids for more space on the queenside.

10...♘e4

10...a5 might block the advance of the a-pawn but it does allow White to continue with ♘a3, heading for the strong outpost of b5.

11 ♕b3

The queen is brought into the action to help increase the pressure on the queenside. In Seirawan-Biyiasas, Lone Pine 1981, White tried 11 a5 to undermine Black's queenside pawns. That game went 11...♖b8 12 ♘a3 (White now brings the knight into the action) 12...cxd4 13 exd4 bxa5 14 ♘c4 (White can win back the pawn and will have long-term pressure against the isolated a-pawn) 14...♗a8 15 ♕c2 ♘b6 16 ♘xa5 e6 17 ♘b3 ♘g5 18 ♘bd2 (the knight on e4 is the key to Black's strategy so White makes an effort to exchange this strong centralised piece) 18...♘xf3+ 19 ♗xf3 ♗xf3 20 ♘xf3 ♖b7 21 c4 ♕d7 22 b3 ♖a8 23 ♖a6 gave White the better chances.

11...a6 12 ♖d1

12 a5 is well met by 12...b5 when the black pawns create a strong barrier.

12...♕c8 13 d5

An intriguing idea to cut off the support of the light-squared bishop which is protecting the knight on e4.

13...♕c7 14 ♘a3 h6 15 ♕c2

White pursues his objective of ousting the knight from the important e4 square.

15...f5 16 ♘h4 ♖f6 17 g4

The next step is to further weaken the support of the knight.

17...♘f8?!

I think 17...♖af8 is an improvement when the game continuation is no use because 18 gxf5 gxf5 19 ♘xf5 allows 19...♘xf2 with a clear advantage. Preferable instead is 19 ♗f4!? with double-edged play.

18 gxf5 gxf5

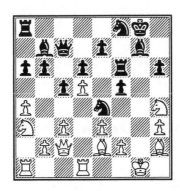

19 ♘xf5!

A clever sacrifice which is a direct result of the strategy to undermine the knight on e4.

19...♖xf5 20 ♕xe4 e6 21 ♗g4

It looks like Black might steal his pawn back but this tactical blow is awkward.

21...♖g5 22 f4 ♗xd5?!

22...♖g6 is necessary although Black's pieces lack harmony.

23 ♖xd5 exd5

Not 23...♖xd5 when White can continue 24 ♗xe6+ ♘xe6 25 ♕xd5 ♖e8 26 f5 and Black is lost.

24 ♕f3 ♖xg4+

24...♖g6 just loses a piece after 25 ♕xd5+ ♕f7 26 ♕xa8.

25 hxg4 ♕f7 26 ♘c4!

The knight rejoins the action with a vengeance! Thanks to the pin on the d-pawn by the queen, at least a pawn can be taken. The game concluded:

26...♖d8 27 ♘xb6 d4 28 cxd4 cxd4 29 e4 ♘e6 30 ♘d5 ♘c7 31 ♘b6 ♘e6 32 ♖f1 d3 33 ♘d5

33 ♕xd3? ♗d4+ wins a piece and suddenly it is Black who is on top.

33...♕a7+ 34 ♔h1 ♕d4 35 ♘e7+ ♔h7 36 ♘c6 ♕c4 37 ♘xd8 ♘d4 38 ♕g2 ♘c2 39 b3 ♕c3 40 e5 d2 41 ♕e4+ ♔h8 42 e6 d5 43 ♕xd5 ♕h3 44 ♖g1 ♕e3 45 ♘f7+ ♔h7 46 g5 1-0

Probably the most popular strategy to combat the London System is to play the queen to e8 in order to facilitate ...e7-e5. I think in this particular case it is right to play an early c2-c4 to help promote a queenside pawn storm.

Raud-Krupenski
Estonian Championship 2001

1 d4 ♘f6 2 ♘f3 g6 3 ♗f4 ♗g7 4 e3 d6 5 h3 0-0 6 ♗e2 ♘bd7 7 0-0 ♕e8

Black wants to play ...e7-e5 which is regarded as the critical variation.

8 c4

I usually try to avoid c2-c4 in my recommended lines but I know from defending the black side that White's pawn storm on the queen's flank is awkward to meet.

8...e5 9 ♗h2 ♕e7

The queen moves up a square to allow the rooks to be co-ordinated. 9...♘e4 is discussed in the next main game.

10 ♘c3 c6

The standard move to maintain the tension by keeping a knight out of b5 or d5. One drawback is that it slightly weakens the pawns on the h2-b8 diagonal.

There is a temptation to ease the pressure on the e5 pawn with 10...e4? but this is premature. For example: 11 ♘d2 ♖e8 (11...b6? 12 ♘cxe4 ♘xe4 13 ♘xe4 is a trick worth knowing because it occurs again and again, Goldstern-Gallagher, Swiss Team Ch 1993) 12 ♘b5! (a good example of how White can take advantage of the absence of a pawn on c6) 12...♕d8 13 c5! (the perfect way to exploit the might of the dark-squared bishop) 13...a6 14 cxd6! axb5 15 dxc7 ♕e7 16 ♗xb5 (White has three pawns for a piece and lots of tactical chances with a pawn on the seventh rank) 16...♗f8 17 ♘c4 ♕e6 18 ♕c2 ♕d5 19 a4 (White's advantage is partly based on his control of the position whereas Black is reduced to reactive defence) 19...♖e6 20 ♖fc1 ♘e8 21 ♕c3 ♘ef6 (21...♘d6? 22 ♗xd7 ♗xd7 23 ♘b6 wins) 22 ♘e5 ♘b6 23 ♘c4 ♘fd7 24 ♕b3 ♖f6 25 ♗xd7 ♘xd7 26 ♕b5! gave White excellent chances and he eventually won, Spassky-Bukić, Bugojno 1978. Alternatively, 10...♖e8 also runs into trouble after the strike 11 c5!, endeavouring to weaken the black pawn structure. The game Lopushnoy-Bratchenko, Kazan 1995, continued: 11...a6 12 ♖c1 e4 13 cxd6 cxd6 14 ♘d2 b5? (a classic error when Black's pawn has advanced to e4) 15 ♘cxe4! ♘d5 (15...♘xe4 16 ♘xe4 ♕xe4 17 ♗f3 pins the queen) 16 ♗f3 and White was a clear pawn up.

11 ♖c1

The queen's rook is brought into the action. Though not regarded as a main line the results of this continuation have been impressive and rely on active piece play rather than large numbers of variations. White can also consider 11 ♕c2 before launching the queenside pawns. For instance: 11...♘e8 12 a3 (12 b4 f5 13 c5 d5 14 dxe5 ♘xe5 15 ♘d4 ♘f6 with equal chances, Portisch-Butnoris, USSR 1969) 12...f5 13 b4 e4 14 ♘d2 ♘df6 15 c5 d5 16 b5 with the initiative, Cavusoglu-Johansson, Varna 2002.

11...a6

Black intends to hinder the progress of white pawns on the queenside by planning ...b7-b5. Black has tried an assortment of alternatives:

a) 11...e4 12 ♘d2 ♖e8 13 b4 a5 14 a3 axb4 15 axb4 gave White the usual queenside space advantage, Johanson-Lane, Canberra 2001.

b) 11...♖d8!? 12 b4 ♘f8 13 ♕b3 exd4 14 exd4 with an edge for White due to his space advantage, Fell-Kimura, Canberra 2001.

c) 11... ♖e8 12 ♖e1 h6 13 b4 ♘h7 14 ♕b3 ♔h8 15 c5 with plenty of queenside play, Nill-Beutel, Regensburg 1996.

d) 11...♘e8 (probably the best of the bunch) 12 b4 f5 13 c5 (or 13 a4 g5 14 c5 gives White a small plus) 13...d5 14 b5 f4?! (14 ...e4!? is a better option) 15 bxc6 bxc6 16 dxe5 fxe3 17 ♘xd5! (bravo) 17...exf2+ 18 ♖xf2 cxd5 19 ♕xd5+ ♕f7 20 ♕xa8 1-0 Borges Mateos-Horcajada Reales, Madrid 2001.

12 b4 b5 13 c5

A simple plan for White is to put a rook on the c-file and then find a way to play c4-c5. The solid nature of White's position usually forces Black to play with great care.

13...dxc5 14 bxc5 ♘e8 15 ♖e1 ♖a7?!

Already Kupenski is not sure how to defend. Though 15...e4 looks a reasonable idea it allows White's dark-squared bishop to take a more active role.

16 ♕b3 ♔h8 17 a4

So far White has not doing anything special except chip away at Black's queenside pawn structure. However it is a policy that has certainly worked wonders because he is already on top.

17...f5 18 axb5 axb5 19 ♘a2

The start of a manoeuvre to target the weak pawn on c6.

19...e4 20 ♘b4 ♖f6

The acceptance of the sacrifice by 20...exf3 allows White all the fun after 21 ♘xc6 ♕g5 22 ♗xf3 ♖b7 23 ♖a1 ♘ef6 24 ♘b4 with a clear advantage.

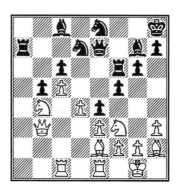

21 ♗d6!

A superb move, which splits the defence into two and allows White to deliver a decisive fork on c6.

21...②xd6 22 ②xc6 ②xc5 23 dxc5 ♕f7 24 ♕xf7 ♖axf7 25 ②fe5 1-0

9...②e4 is often played because it is recommended in old books on the basis of a drawn game from the 1970s. But time has moved on and here White finds a way to create problems by a surprising queen sortie.

Payen-Gross
New York 1999

1 d4 ②f6 2 ②f3 g6 3 ♗f4 ♗g7 4 e3 d6 5 h3 0-0 6 ♗e2 ②bd7 7 0-0 ♕e8 8 ♗h2 e5 9 c4 ②e4

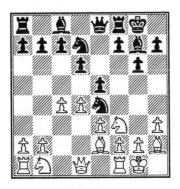

The knight moves to allow Black to exert greater influence on the d4 pawn by uncovering the diagonal of the king's bishop.

10 ②bd2
In keeping with the standard plan of the London System the queen's knight is developed on d2.

10...②xd2
A teenage Garry Kasparov successfully dealt with 10...f5 in a game against Negulescu, Cagnes 1977, by continuing 11 dxe5 ②xd2 12 ♕xd2 dxe5 13 ♖ad1 ♕e7 14 c5!? (a typically energetic move from Kasparov) 14...e4 (or 14...②xc5 15 ♗xe5 ♗xe5 16 ♕d5+ ♗e6 17 ♕xe5 with an edge) 15 c6! (White is happy to give away a pawn because Black will have a hard task defending the extra material) 15...bxc6 16 ②d4 ②e5 17 ♕a5 c5 18 ②b5 ♖f7 19 ②xc7! ♖b8 (19...♕xc7 20 ♖d8+ ♗f8 21 ♕xc7 ♖xc7 22 ♗xe5 wins) 20 ②d5 ♕f8 21 ②f6+ ♗xf6 22 ♗xe5 with the better chances.

11 ♕xd2 e4

One way of stemming the forthcoming queenside pawn rush is 11...a5 when Dunnington-Kleinplatz, Toulouse 1993, continued 12 ♕c2 ♕e7 13 ♖ac1 ♖e8 14 c5 (once again in this system the c-pawn is advanced to undermine the black pawn chain) 14...dxc5 15 dxc5 ♘b8 16 ♖fd1 ♗d7 17 ♗g3 ♗f6 18 ♘d2 intending ♘e4 with a slight plus.

12 ♘e1 ♕e7

Or 12...f5 13 ♘c2 g5 14 ♕a5! (an important queen manoeuvre to provoke weaknesses on the queenside—which is mirrored in the main game. 14 ♖ac1 is also possible when 14...♕g6 15 c5 dxc5 16 ♗xc7 ♔h8 17 ♖fd1 led to roughly equal play, Dizdar-Petrosian, Jurmala 1983) 14 ...♕d8 15 f4 exf3 16 ♖xf3 (16 ♗xf3!?) 16...♘f6 17 ♗d3 b6 18 ♕e1 ♕e8 19 ♕e2 ♘e4 20 ♖e1 ♗d7 21 ♘b4 ♗e6 22 ♘d5 ½-½ Speelman-Sax, Lucerne 1982.

13 ♘c2 f5

13...♘b6 has been suggested but I think the knight just gets in the way on the queenside and offers an easy target for White's advancing pawns. For example: 14 a4 a5 15 ♘a3 (now that there is no a-pawn to police the b5 outpost, the white knight can occupy this square) 15...♗d7 16 ♘b5 ♖fc8 when Black is already on the defensive, Koch-Hoffman, ICCF Email 2001.

14 ♕a5!

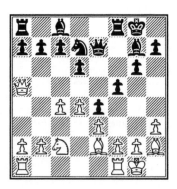

I like this move which threatens the c7 pawn and allows the queen to support the further advance of the c-pawn. It is an important improvement on 14 b4, played in the game Yusupov-Tukmakov, USSR 1978, and recommended as the best way to continue in older opening books. There play proceeded 14...g5 15 c5 ♘f6 16 ♘a3 f4! 17 exf4 g4 and Black had pretty good kingside play although the game was drawn in 30 moves.

14...♘f6

The knight moves, uncovering the black queen's protection of the c7 pawn. Instead 14...♕d8 might seem a retrograde step but is probably the right way to proceed even if 15 ♖fd1, angling for a timely c4-c5, does give

White a small edge. On the other hand after 14...b6?? would be a big blunder because of 15 ♕d5+.

15 c5

This advance, increasing the influence of the dark-squared bishop, can be seen time and again in games in this chapter. Knowledge of this plan can take you a long way into the middlegame.

15...g5 16 cxd6 cxd6 17 ♘a3 b5?

A reckless attempt to slow down White's progress on the queenside and gain time to get on with his own counterattack on the other flank. Such weakening moves are often made by impatient King's Indian players in the name of tactics—such as here where Black wants to advance ...f4 without allowing ♕xg5.

18 ♕b4 ♘e8 19 ♗xb5 f4 20 ♗xe8 ♕xe8 21 ♕xd6

White is two pawns up while Black's attack is still a long way off. The game concluded:

21...♗a6 22 ♖fc1 fxe3 23 fxe3 ♕f7 24 ♗g3 ♖ad8 25 ♖c7 ♕f1+ 26 ♖xf1 ♖xf1+ 27 ♔h2 ♖xd6 28 ♗xd6 ♖e1 29 ♘c2 ♖e2 30 ♘b4 ♗d3 31 ♘d5 ♖c2 32 ♖xa7 ♗f1 33 ♗e5 ♗xe5+ 34 dxe5 ♗xg2 35 ♘f6+ ♔f8 36 e6 1-0

SUMMARY

Payen-Popovych is an opportunity to see what White should do against a double fianchetto. A sterner test of White's resources arises in **Kudischewitsch-Murey** where Black strikes out with a quick ...c5. A fairly level middlegame eventually turns in White's favour after the support of Black's influential knight on e4 is cleverly chipped away. The plan of ...♕e8 followed by ...e7-e5 must be treated with respect. **Raud-Krupenski** sees White playing a quick c2-c4 as a way of speeding up his queenside pawn storm. **Payen-Gross** covers the fashionable 9...♘e4. The spirited reply 14 ♕a5 is hardly mentioned anywhere but in practice it presents Black with real problems.

THE BARRY ATTACK

There is a certain satisfaction in winning a game in style with an opening that has a silly name. The Barry Attack is the perfect weapon for those who open with the queen's pawn, who have to cope with that four-letter word called work and who have neither the time to look at the Internet for the latest theoretical innovations nor the dedication to memorise heaps of book analysis. The Barry will suit people who prefer to fight a kingside fianchetto, especially the King's Indian Defence, without using the London System.

HISTORY OF THE BARRY

The main opening idea has been known for some time: **1 d4 ♘f6 2 ♘f3 g6 3 ♘c3 d5 4 ♗f4**, which was played in the 1920s by Capablanca. The difference in the modern treatment is that the game usually continues **4...♗g7 5 e3 0-0** and now, instead of the quiet 6 h3, with the new move **6 ♗e2** which has revitalised the line.

Apparently the Bangladeshi grandmaster Murshed tried it at the Lloyds Bank tournament in London during the 1980s and it suddenly set a trend. Subsequently this adventurous continuation has been particularly popular in England with Hebden and Hodgson amongst many players who have successfully employed it at the highest level. The leading openings expert John Nunn failed to cope with the 'Barry' against Hebden at Hastings 1996/97. After his defeat Nunn was none too happy and his complaint, which I am happy to quote, should ironically be considered an advert for offbeat lines. Nunn wrote, "Unfortunately, the opening was the so-called 'Barry Attack'. It is quite a good idea to give your favourite opening a ridiculous name, because if someone does lose to it then they have to admit not only that they lost, but that they did so to the 'Monkey's Bum', 'Toilet Variation', 'Barry Attack' or whatever, thereby compounding their misery and making them more apprehensive about the next game." Wise words indeed, which were no doubt echoing in Hebden's head when he repeated the Barry against Nunn the following year at Hastings. And again Nunn lost—in 23 moves!

So, after you too have scored a few victories with this opening, your depressed opponent will perhaps try to find out some history on the Barry but will search in vain—even the prestigious *Oxford Companion to Chess* makes no mention of it. Chess historian Ken Whyld went so far as to make a nationwide appeal in *British Chess Magazine* to find out the origin of the name, but without success. One enterprising person ventured that it might have been named after the Welsh town, perhaps having been played there at a weekend tournament. Ken admitted that he had always assumed "... it was named after John Barry (1873-1940), a strong Bostonian, and was therefore not a joke name." It should come as no surprise that no games appeared to prove the theory. The truth is stranger than fiction. I recall that when Hebden was trying to demonstrate the merits of the opening to other English players in the 1980s, the imaginative idea of ♗e2 followed by an unlikely looking h4 caused many people to claim it was all bluff. Indeed, the Barry is just English slang for a rubbish attack! I hasten to add that nowadays Black fears it.

IDEAS BEHIND THE OPENING

The move-order is an important feature of the opening because it is designed to particularly frustrate King's Indian players. After **1 d4 ♘f6 2 ♘f3 g6 3 ♘c3** the following position is reached.

At this point the King's Indian player is left in a dilemma because the obvious 3...♗g7 allows 4 e4 transposing to the Pirc, where it is highly likely

likely that Black will lack specialised knowledge. Therefore 3...d5 is played to reduce White's control of the centre but this in turn leaves the e5 square ripe for White to install a knight. All this will be alien territory for a King's Indian player who is used to having a pawn on d6. The line is similar to the London System in that a bishop is developed to f4 and White plants a knight on e5. The modern twist is that in some variations White can introduce a different way of handling the position by opting for a quick h2-h4 to initiate a kingside attack.

Hebden-Birnboim

Rishon le Zion 1992

1 d4 ♘f6 2 ♘f3 g6 3 ♘c3 d5

A natural response because White intends to play 4 e4. Pirc practitioners might be tempted to play 3... ♗g7 but Black should be careful because after 4 e4 ♗g7 White can play 5 ♗e3 transposing to the notorious 150 Attack, which I cover in the next chapter.

4 ♗f4 ♗g7 5 e3

5...0-0

At this early stage of the game it is easy to go wrong as those who have played 5...♘bd7?? will confirm—because after 6 ♘b5 Black can resign! And chasing the bishop is obvious but not very good. For example: 5...♘h5?! 6 ♗g5 h6 7 ♗h4 g5 8 ♘e5! (the loose knight on h5 allows White to seize the initiative) 8...♗xe5 9 dxe5 ♘g7 10 ♗g3 ♗e6 11 h4! ♖g8 12 hxg5 hxg5 13 e4 gives White the advantage thanks to the knight on g7 which is no more than a spectator.

6 ♗e2 b6

Black wants to continue his development with a queenside fianchetto. The main alternatives 6...c5, 6...c6 and 6...♗g4 are examined later in the chapter.

7 ♘e5 ♝b7 8 h4

This is the real point of the opening—White can suddenly launch a king-side attack. The idea is that the preliminary ♝e2 aids the advance h5 and the potentially open h-file can be exploited by leaving the rook on h1 and castling queenside.

8...h6

It is not easy to deter White from his aggressive intentions. In the game Rogers-Pribyl, Tallinn 1985, Black tried 8...♘bd7 to exchange one of the attacking pieces, but White obtained a formidable initiative: 9 h5! ♘xe5 10 dxe5 ♘d7?! (10...♘e4 is an improvement although White has good chances after 11 ♝d3 intending ♕f3) 11 hxg6 fxg6 12 ♝d3 (the plan is simply to transfer the queen to the h-file and then checkmate) 12...e6 13 ♕g4 (the queen is on its way) 13...♘c5 14 ♕h3 (the power of controlling the open h-file is evident) 14...♘xd3+ 15 cxd3 ♔f7 16 ♘b5 ♕e7 17 ♖c1 ♖fc8 18 ♔e2 ♝a6 19 ♘d4 c5 20 ♘f3 h6 21 ♝xh6 ♖h8 22 ♘g5+ ♔e8 23 ♕xe6 ♕xe6 24 ♘xe6 ♝xe5 25 ♝f4 ♔e7 26 ♖xh8 1-0

9 h5 g5

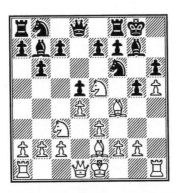

10 ♗xg5

White attempts to rip apart Black's kingside defences after only 10 moves! The idea is to follow up with an advance of the h-pawn leaving Black's king vulnerable to a lightning attack. In Balashov-Belov, St Petersburg 1998, White tried 10 ♗g3 rejecting glorious sacrifices and finding another route to victory. The game continued 10...c5 11 f4 (White wants to break Black's defensive pawn barrier) 11...gxf4 12 ♗xf4 ♘bd7 13 0-0 ♘xe5 14 ♗xe5 ♘h7 15 ♗xg7 ♔xg7 16 ♕e1 ♘g5 17 ♕g3 ♕b8 18 ♖f4 (the obvious plan is to double rooks and increase the kingside pressure) 18...♕d6 19 ♖af1 ♖ae8 20 ♘b5 ♕b8 21 c4 e5 22 ♖f6 exd4 23 ♘d6! ♖xe3 24 ♖xf7+ ♖xf7 25 ♘f5+ ♖xf5 26 ♕xb8 wins.

10...hxg5 11 h6 ♗h8

The bishop retreats leaving the black king with little room to manoeuvre. In the game Stefanova-Del Mundo, Las Vegas 1997, Black tried 11...♗xh6 and after 12 ♖xh6 ♔g7 13 ♖h3 ♖h8 14 ♖g3 White had a clear advantage.

12 h7+

12...♘xh7 looks logical but White has all the fun after 13 ♗a6! which clears a path for the queen to enter the fray. For example: 13...♗c8 14 ♗xc8 (the simplest but for 'show offs' 14 ♕h5 ♗f5 15 ♗d3 ♕c8 and now the startling 16 ♘g6! leads to mate) 14...♕xc8 15 ♕h5 ♕f5 16 g4 ♕xc2 17 e4 winning.

12...♔g7 13 ♗d3

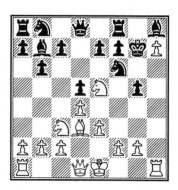

A great position to achieve straight from the opening.

13...♗a6

In his bid to survive, Black wants to exchange one of the attacking pieces.

13...c5 was shown to be weak after 14 ♕f3 ♕c8 15 ♗f5 e6 16 ♕h3 with a winning position, Van Kerkhof-Broekmeulen, Kaatsheuvel 2000. A sterner defence is 13...e6 but after 14 ♕f3 ♖e8 15 ♕h3 ♔f8 16 ♕h6+ ♔e7

17 ♕xg5 (White has two pawns for the piece, a strong pawn on the seventh rank, and a raging attack) 17...♖f8 18 ♘e2 ♘bd7 19 ♘f4 gave White good compensation for the piece, Bannink-Uhlmann, Dresden 1999.

14 ♕f3

The queen joins in the onslaught and the defence is difficult because Black's pieces lack harmony.

14...♗xd3 15 cxd3 ♕d6 16 ♕f5 ♖d8 17 ♕xg5+ ♔f8 18 ♔e2!

A star move. The king steps forward to allow the queen's rook to reinforce the attack.

18...a6 19 ♖h6 ♘bd7 20 ♖ah1 ♕e6 21 ♖1h4

The idea is 22 ♖g4 when 22...♘xg4 is no help due to 23 ♕g8 mate.

21...♘xe5 22 dxe5 ♔e8 23 exf6 exf6 24 ♕g3 ♔e7 25 ♕xc7+ ♖d7 26 ♕g3 ♖c8 1-0

So what was the game that caused John Nunn such embarrassment? The answer is the following miniature where Black's prepared improvement leads ultimately to disaster.

Hebden-Nunn

Hastings 1997/98

1 d4 ♘f6 2 ♘f3 g6 3 ♘c3 d5 4 ♗f4 ♗g7 5 e3 0-0 6 ♗e2 c5 7 ♘e5

This is a typical manoeuvre in the opening and keeps White's options open, depending on how Black responds. The quiet 7 0-0 is examined in the next main game. Instead 7 dxc5 is a simple alternative, e.g. 7...♕a5 8 ♘d2 (White wants to have more of a say on the queenside and can do this by chasing the black queen) 8...♕xc5 9 ♘b3 ♕b6 10 a4!? (a good idea because after Black blocks any further advance of the pawn White will have more control over the b5 square) 10...a5 11 ♘b5 (White has a nagging edge thanks to his well placed pieces) 11...♘a6 12 0-0 ♗d7 13 ♗e5 ♖fc8 14 c3 ♗c6? 15 ♗d4! ♛d8 16 ♘a7 and White must win material, Barsov-Joshi, Aden 2002.

7...cxd4

Black eases the tension in the centre. This is a major crossroads for Black so it deserves more analysis than usual:

a) 7...♗e6 8 0-0 ♘bd7 9 a4 ♖c8 10 a5 with a slight plus, Hebden-R.Pert, British Ch 2002.

b) 7...♘c6 8 0-0 and now:

b1) 8...cxd4 (8...♛b6? fails to 9 ♘a4 winning a pawn) 9 exd4 and now:

b11) 9...♛b6 10 ♘xc6 bxc6 11 ♘a4 ♛a5 12 c3 ♘d7 (12...♗a6!? 13 ♘c5 ♘h5! 14 ♗e3 ♗xe2 15 ♛xe2 e5 offers equal chances) 13 b4 ♛d8 14 ♛d2 e5 15 ♗h6 ♗xh6 16 ♛xh6 ♖e8 (16...a5!? has been suggested) 17 ♖fe1 ♖b8 18 dxe5 ♖xe5 19 ♛d2 gave White a slight plus in Hebden-Nunn, Hastings 1996/97.

b12) 9...♘d7 10 ♘f3 ♘b6 11 h3 f6 (Black intends to play ...e7-e5) 12 a4 a5 (12...e5 is well met by 13 a5) 13 ♗b5 ♗f5 14 ♖e1 ♘b4 15 ♖c1 ♖c8 16 ♛e2 with equal chances, Hebden-Akesson, Isle Of Man 2000.

b2) 8...♗f5!? 9 ♘a4 cxd4 10 ♘xc6 bxc6 11 exd4 ♘d7 (or 11...♘e4 12 c3 ♖e8 13 ♗a6 ♘d6 14 ♖e1 ♗c8 15 ♗f1 a5 16 ♘c5 gave White the better game in Hebden-Ghasi, Bradford 2001) 12 c3 ♖e8 13 ♖e1 e5 14 ♗e3 led to a roughly level position in Hebden-Lalić, British Ch 2001.

8 exd4 ♘fd7

This is what Nunn had planned to improve on his previous game with Hebden. The idea is simple enough—to exchange an attacking piece.

9 ♘f3 ♘f6 10 ♘e5 ♘fd7 11 ♘f3 ♘f6 12 ♛d2

Hebden told me that Nunn had been expecting an early draw here—but after the text they merely exchanged knowing smiles and got on with it.

12...♗g4 13 ♘e5 ♗xe2 14 ♕xe2 ♘h5 15 ♗e3 ♘c6 16 0-0-0 ♖c8 17 f4

The knight is well supported on e5 and White can now start a major pawn advance on the kingside.

17...♘f6 18 g4 ♕a5 19 a3!

There is no point in allowing 19...♘b4.

19...♘xe5 20 fxe5 ♖xc3?

This looks good but there is a big hole in Black's analysis. A better idea is 20...♘d7 but White still has a slight advantage. Meanwhile the double-edged nature of the position is apparent after 20...♘e4 when 21 ♘xe4 dxe4 22 h4 f6 23 h5 once again gives White a strong attack.

21 exf6 ♖fc8

Black adds a rook to the attack. Instead, 21...♖xa3 22 bxa3 ♕xa3+ 23 ♔d2 ♗xf6 24 ♖b1 or 21...♖xe3 22 ♕xe3 ♗xf6 23 g5 both leave White on top.

22 ♔b1!

A cool move. Black is completely busted because too many pieces are hanging. Apparently Black was expecting 22 bxc3 when 22...♕xa3+ leads to a draw after 23 ♔d2 ♕xc3+ 24 ♔c1 ♕a3+. If 22 fxg7 then 22...♖xa3! 23 bxa3 ♕xa3+ once again leads to perpetual check.

22...♖xc2 23 ♖d2 1-0

Black resigned in view of 23...♖xd2 24 ♗xd2 and, after the black queen moves, White takes on g7 leaving him with an extra piece.

If White thinks that Black might latch on to an improvement then it is possible to deviate as early as move 7.

S.Pedersen-Leskiewicz
Gausdal 2000

1 d4 ♘f6 2 ♘f3 g6 3 ♘c3 d5 4 ♗f4 ♗g7 5 e3 0-0 6 ♗e2 c5 7 0-0

Instead of castling queenside and coming out with all guns blazing, White chooses a quiet but sound alternative.

7...cxd4 8 exd4 ♘c6 9 ♘e5 ♘d7!?

9...♗f5!? should also be considered.

10 ♘xd5 ♘cxe5 11 dxe5 ♘xe5 12 ♖e1 e6

The Australian is making life difficult for himself by not curbing White's slight initiative. 12...♗e6! is the best way to seek equality.

13 ♗b5 ♗d7?! 14 ♗xe5 ♗xb5

If 14...♗xe5 White is better after 15 ♗xd7 ♗xb2 (15...♕xd7 16 ♘f6+ wins) 16 ♖b1 ♗g7 17 ♕xd5.

15 ♗xg7 ♔xg7 16 ♕d4+ ♔h6

After 16...♔g8 White has all the fun by 17 ♘f6+ ♔h8 18 ♕e5! intending ♘g4+ among other threats.

17 ♖e3!

The wandering black king is enough encouragement for White to sacrifice a piece and go on a king-hunt.

17...exd5 18 ♖h3+ ♔g5 19 ♖e1 h5 20 ♕e3+ 1-0

One of Black's most popular replies is an early ...c6 to meet ♘e5 with ...♘fd7 when there is no pawn on c5 to worry about. Dunnington's approach with 7 h3 offers White the chance to exert a positional squeeze.

Dunnington-Valensi

Cannes 1992

1 ♘f3 ♘f6 2 d4 g6 3 ♘c3 d5 4 ♗f4 ♗g7 5 e3 0-0 6 ♗e2 c6

A quiet move which strengthens d5 and makes way for a timely ...♕b6.

7 h3

A positional response to give the white-squared bishop an escape square on h2 and stop ...♗g4.

7...♘bd7 8 0-0 ♖e8 9 ♗h2

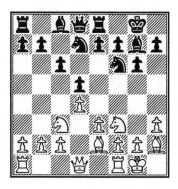

Posing Black the question: how to continue? The plan is ...e5 but this is difficult to realise. If 9...♘h5 10 g4 maintains White's space advantage. This is the reason for White's text move as the passive 9 ♖e1 would allow Black to respond with 9...♘h5 10 ♗h2 e5 11 g4 exd4 12 exd4 ♘f6 after which White emerges from the opening with no advantage.

9...♘e4

Black experimented with 9...♘b6 in Dunnington-Ahn, Eupen 1993, preferring to seek play on the queenside. There followed 10 ♗d3 (aiming to break in the centre with e4) 10...♘c4? 11 ♗xc4 dxc4 12 ♘e5 b5 (there is no good way to defend the pawn as 12...♗e6 is trumped by 13 ♕e2 renewing the pressure on c4) 13 ♘xc6 ♕b6 14 ♘e5 leaving White a clear pawn ahead.

10 ♘xe4 dxe4 11 ♘g5 e5?

Black opts for active piece play but should prefer 11...♘f6 when 12 ♗c4 ♖f8 13 f3 gives White the better game.

12 ♘xe4 exd4 13 ♘d6 ♖f8 14 exd4 ♕b6 15 c3 ♕xb2 16 ♕d3 ♕a3 17 ♗g4! c5

The alternative 17...f5 blocks the diagonal but it merely exposes the king after 18 ♕c4+ ♔h8 19 ♗f3 when 19...h6 loses to 20 ♘f7+ ♔h7 21 ♗d6.

18 ♘xc8 ♖fxc8 19 ♗xd7

Dunnington is a whole piece up and soon wraps up victory:

19...♖d8 20 ♕b5 cxd4 21 cxd4 ♕e7 22 ♗g4 ♗xd4 23 ♖ae1 ♕a3 24 ♗c7 ♖f8 25 ♖d1 ♗c5 26 ♖d3 a6 27 ♕c4 ♕b4 28 ♕xb4 ♗xb4 29 ♖b1 1-0

Black's light-squared bishop is often passive so it makes sense to try and exchange it for a potential attacking piece.

Wirthensohn-Antognini
Swiss Championship 2001

1 d4 ♘f6 2 ♘f3 g6 3 ♘c3 d5 4 ♗f4 ♗g7 5 e3 0-0 6 ♗e2 ♗g4

Black develops his bishop with the aim of exchanging one of the potential attacking pieces. It is a popular choice because sometimes the light-squared bishop ends up in a passive role while White gets on with the job of attacking the kingside.

7 ♘e5 ♗xe2 8 ♕xe2

8...c6

The c-pawn is advanced to protect d5 and allow the queen to emerge on a5 in some variations to attack the white king after it castles queenside. 8...c5 is also possible to challenge the centre. Play might continue:

a) 9 h4 (an attacking move in keeping with the standard plan) 9...cxd4 10 exd4 ♘c6 11 0-0-0 ♖c8 12 h5 ♘e4? 13 ♘xe4 dxe4 14 hxg6 fxg6 (or 14...hxg6 15 ♕e3 ♘b4 16 ♕h3 wins) 15 ♕c4+ ♔h8 16 ♘xg6 mate 1-0 Stumpf-Bruns, Bad Wörishofen 2000.

b) 9 ♕b5 (White is in the hunt for pawns) 9...cxd4 (or 9...♕b6 10 dxc5 ♕xb5 11 ♘xb5 ♖c8 12 ♘d3 ♘a6 13 b4 allows White to hold on to the extra pawn) 10 exd4 ♘c6 (perhaps 10...b6 should be considered when 11 0-0 e6 12 ♖fe1 gives White a slight edge.) 11 ♕xb7 ♘xd4 12 0-0-0! ♖b8 13 ♕xa7 ♘b5 14 ♘xb5 ♖xb5 15 ♘c6 ♕a8 (15...♕e8 is hardly an improvement after 16 ♘xe7+ ♔h8 17 ♖he1 giving White a winning advantage) 16 ♘xe7+ ♔h8 17 ♕xa8 ♖xa8 18 ♗e5 ♖xa2 19 c4 ♖b7 20 ♔b1 ♖axb2+ 21 ♗xb2 ♘e4 22 ♖xd5 and Black is busted, Hebden-McDonald, British Ch 1991.

9 h4 ♘bd7

Black gets another piece into the action and proposes an exchange of the dominant knight on e5. The miniature Semrl-Grilc, Ljubljana 2000, ended in a bizarre finish after 9...♕a5 10 0-0-0 b5 (10...♘bd7 is met by 11 h5!) 11·a3 b4 12 axb4 ♕a1+? (amazingly this is the losing move—12...♕xb4 was necessary when 13 g4 offers equal chances) 13 ♔d2 ♕xb2 14 ♘d3 1-0.

10 0-0-0

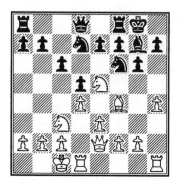

10...♘xe5

It is not easy to see how Black should conduct the defence and this has led to Black trying various ideas, albeit with little success:

a) 10...♘h5 does little to stop the kingside advance. For instance: 11 g4 ♘xf4 12 exf4 e6 13 h5 f6? (13...c5!? at least tries to generate counterplay on the queenside) 14 ♘xg6! ♖e8 (accepting the sacrifice is fatal: 14...hxg6 15 ♕xe6+ ♔h7 16 hxg6+ ♔xg6 17 f5+ ♔g5 18 ♕e3+ ♔xg4 19 ♖dg1+ ♔xf5 20 ♖h5 mate) 15 h6 hxg6 16 hxg7 ♔xg7 17 ♕e3 f5 18 g5 ♕e7 19 ♖h3 ♖h8 20 ♖dh1 ♖ag8 21 ♘e2 ♕e8 22 ♕a3! (now that Black is tied up on the kingside, White is eager to infiltrate on the queen's flank) 22...♖xh3 23 ♖xh3 a6 24 ♕d6 ♕f7 25 ♕c7 ♕e7 26 ♘g1 ♖e8 27 ♘f3 ♔g8 28 ♕xb7 ♖b8 29 ♕xc6 1-0 Hebden-Williams, Swansea 1995.

b) 10...♖c8 11 h5 ♖e8 (11...♘xh5 is met by 12 ♖xh5 gxh5 13 ♕xh5 with a strong attack) 12 hxg6 fxg6 13 ♕f3 ♘f8 14 g4 b5 15 ♗h6 (the threat is 16 g5) 15...♘8d7 16 ♗xg7 ♔xg7 17 g5 ♘xe5 18 gxf6+ exf6 19 dxe5 fxe5 20 ♖xh7+! ♔xh7 21 ♕f7+ ♔h6 22 ♖h1+ ♔g5 23 ♖g1+ 1-0 Hebden-Fox, Hastings 1995.

11 ♗xe5 ♘d7?!

Black retreats in order to get rid of the influential bishop on e5 though this also means that for the time being the black king is lacking defenders. Hebden-Ivanov, Halkidiki 2000 saw 11...b5 12 h5 b4 (or 12...♘xh5 13 g4 ♘f6 14 ♕f3 intending ♕h3 with a good attack) 13 ♘b1 ♕d7 14 ♘d2 ♘e4 15 ♘xe4 dxe4 16 ♗xg7 ♔xg7 17 f4 which led to double-edged play.

12 ♗xg7 ♔xg7 13 e4

Now that White has exchanged the key defensive bishop on g7, the next stage is to open the position to make it easier to direct the pieces towards the black king.

13...dxe4 14 ♘xe4 e6 15 g4

Having no fear of counterplay on the queen's flank Wirthensohn can provoke new weaknesses with a kingside pawn storm.

15...♘f6 16 ♘g3 ♕d6 17 g5 ♕f4+ 18 ♔b1 ♘d5 19 ♘e4

The fluent attack is easy to play because White has the pleasant options of c2-c4, to enable a white knight to take up residence on f6, or simply h4-h5.

19...♖ad8 20 h5 b6 21 ♖dg1 f5?

It is hardly surprising that Black buckles under the pressure of trying to get rid of the strong central knight. Instead 21...♖h8 22 ♖g4 ♕c7 23 ♕f3 is very good for White.

22 gxf6+ ♘xf6 23 ♘g5!

The killer knight fork on e6 decides the outcome of the game.

23...♖fe8 24 ♘xe6+ ♖xe6 25 ♕xe6 ♖e8 26 ♕xc6 ♕xd4 27 ♕c7+ ♔g8 28 hxg6 1-0

SUMMARY

The modern idea of ♘e5 followed by h2-h4 worked well in the game **Hebden-Birnboim**, where White wins a fantastic brilliancy. It was known as the 'game of vengeance' when **Hebden-Nunn** was played at Hastings —but Black's vow to beat the opening that had caught him out previously ended in disaster. 6...c5 is given another outing in **S.Pedersen-Leskiewicz** with White adopting a less confrontational approach. Another idea is 6...c6 to strengthen the d5-pawn and this is examined in the game **Dunnington-Valensi** where Black shows how easy it is to go wrong in what seems to be a tranquil position. 6...♗g4 is one way to solve the problem of what to do with the light-squared bishop and in the game **Wirthensohn-Antognini** Black is happy to exchange pieces in a bid to thwart the potential attack.

The Barry Attack is worth a go at any level!

THE 150 ATTACK

The 150 Attack is primarily a 1 e4 opening arising after the moves **1 e4 d6 2 d4 ♞f6 3 ♞c3 g6 4 ♝e3 ♝g7 5 ♞f3 0-0 6 ♛d2** and is regarded as a sharp system against the Pirc. Our interest lies in the fact that it can also occur via the Barry Attack: 1 d4 ♞f6 2 ♞f3 g6 3 ♞c3 and now if Black plays 3…g6 then 4 e4 will transpose to the Pirc, enabling White to play the 150 Attack. I have made it easier for 1 d4 players by changing the original move-order to show how playing the Barry Attack can allow White to play the 150.

HISTORY OF THE 150 ATTACK

In the late 1980s a new generation of English players started to experiment with a sharp line against the Pirc, the main idea of which was to play ♝e3, ♛d2, ♝h6, followed by h4-h5 to open the h-file for the white's king's rook and deliver mate. Of course, this seemed too good to be true and was rapidly dubbed the 150 Attack (a peculiarity of the English grading system is that 150 translates to an 1800 Elo rating) because it seemed that only a club player would employ such a blatantly obvious attacking idea and expect to succeed. However a look at the games of Adams, Dunnington, Emms, Hebden, Hodgson, Jacobs, and Lane, to name just a few, saw outstanding results and the trend has spread worldwide. There have been various refinements—mainly whether to play an early f2-f3 or ♞f3. Of course our repertoire via 1 d4 dictates that we look at the ♞f3 option.

IDEAS BEHIND THE OPENING

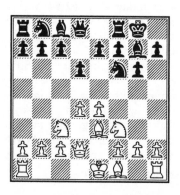

This is the position which White is aiming for in the opening. The idea is to exchange Black's key defensive bishop by ♗h6, castle queenside and then advance the kingside pawns. Of course, depending on Black's set-up, White can also castle kingside and play a steady system with possibilities of tactical chances.

Spraggett-Gonzalez Amaya
Seville 2002

1 d4 ♘f6 2 ♘f3 g6 3 ♘c3 ♗g7 4 e4 d6

Black discourages 5 e5 which is now met by 5...dxe5 6 dxe5 ♕xd1+ 7 ♘xd1 ♘g4 8 ♗f4 ♘c6 with equality.

5 ♗e3 0-0 6 ♕d2

The ideal position mentioned in the introduction to this chapter has now been reached. It should be noted that the original move-order was 1 e4 g6 2 d4 ♗g7 3 ♘c3 d6 4 ♗e3 ♘f6 5 ♘f3 0-0 6 ♕d2.

6...♘bd7

Black gets on with the job of developing in the standard Pirc style by preparing to play ...e7-e5. There are various alternatives:

a) 6...e5 and now

a1) 7 dxe5 dxe5 8 0-0-0 ♕e7 9 ♘d5 (9 h4!? is a possibility) 9...♘xd5 10 ♕xd5 ♘d7 11 ♕a5 b6 12 ♕a4 ♘f6 13 ♗b5 ♗b7 14 ♗c6 ♗xc6 15 ♕xc6 ♕e8 with equal chances, Hebden-Carlier, Noyon 2001.

a2) 7 ♗d3 ♘g4 8 ♗g5 ♘f6 9 dxe5 dxe5 10 0-0-0 (10 ♘xe5! ♖e8 11 ♘f3 ♗g4 12 0-0-0 leaves White a pawn up) 10...♗g4 11 ♕e3 c6 12 ♗c4 with an edge for White, A.Silson-G.Smit, Newcastle 2000.

b) 6...♘g4 7 ♗g5 f6!? (an idea proposed by Gufeld to fend off White's intended exchange of dark-squared bishops) 8 ♗h4 ♘c6 9 h3 ♘h6 10 0-0-0 (White's middlegame plan is simply to develop and then see how Black intends to mobilize his awkward-looking kingside pieces) 10...♘f7 11 ♔b1 ♗h6 12 ♕e1 ♗d7 13 ♗c4 e5? (a natural but losing move) 14 dxe5 1-0 Lane-Reilly, Canberra 2001.

c) 6...a6 (Black intends to keep his options open by preparing ...b7-b5 and threatening ...b5-b4 to remove the defender of the e4 pawn) 7 ♗h6 b5 8 ♗d3 (White defends the e4 pawn against the threat ...b5-b4) 8...♗b7 9 ♗xg7 ♔xg7 10 e5 ♘fd7 11 ♗e4 (11 h4 is an aggressive idea when 11...dxe5 12 h5 ♖h8 13 0-0-0 exd4?! 14 ♗e4 is better for White) 11...♗xe4 12 ♘xe4 d5 13 ♘g3 e6 14 h4 h6 15 h5 g5 16 ♘h2 gave White good attacking chances and eventual victory in Hebden-Sutovsky, Isle of Man 2000.

d) 6...♗g4 7 ♘g5 ♘c6 (7...h6? 8 h3 ♗h5 9 ♘xf7! ♖xf7 10 g4 is good for White) 8 d5 and now:

d1) 8...♘b8 9 f3 ♗d7 (if 9...h6 then 10 fxg4 hxg5 11 ♗e2 ♘h7 12 0-0-0 gives White a strong attack) 10 h4 h5 (White's attacking possibilities are revealed after 10...h6 11 ♘h3 h5 12 ♗h6 with an edge or 10...c6 11 h5! ♘xh5 12 ♘xh7! ♔xh7 13 g4 with the advantage) 11 g4! c6 (11...hxg4 12 h5!? ♘xh5 13 fxg4 ♗xg4 14 ♗e2 with attacking chances according to Khalifman) 12 gxh5 ♘xh5 13 0-0-0 ♕a5 14 ♗d4 ♗xd4?! 15 ♕xd4 with the brighter prospects, Khalifman-Adams, Lucerne 1997.

d2) 8...♘b4 9 f3 ♗d7 10 a3 (Khalifman suggests 10 ♘d1!? ♘a6 11 h4 as a way to accelerate the attack) 10...♘a6 11 h4 h6 12 ♘h3 ♗xh3 13 ♖xh3 h5 14 0-0-0 ♕c8 15 ♗e2 c5 16 g4 with a similar attack to the main game, Tissir-Marin, Cairo 2001.

7 ♗h6

The Canadian grandmaster wants to exchange bishops because the one on g7 is an important kingside defender.

7...e5

If Black delays striking out at the centre then White can simply carry on attacking. In the game Fernandez Baldor-Rudareanu Ioan, Aviles 2001, Black tried 7...c6 but soon buckled under the pressure: 8 0-0-0 b5 9 ♗d3 a5 10 h4 (White goes for the blatant but rewarding 150 attack) 10...♘b6 11 h5 ♘xh5? 12 ♖xh5! winning because 12...gxh5 allows 13 ♕g5 with mate to follow.

8 0-0-0 ♗xh6

After Black has already castled kingside it is probably not a good idea to invite the white queen into the heart of his position. Kupreichik-Reichwald, Bad Wörishofen 2001, saw 8...exd4 as a way for the knights to strike the e4 pawn: 9 ♘xd4 ♘c5 10 ♗xg7 ♔xg7 11 f3 (now the threat to e4 has passed White can go on the offensive) 11...♗d7 12 g4 a6 13 h4 h5 (it seems that Black has put a stop to White's kingside ambitions but is soon overcome in instructive fashion) 14 ♗e2 b5 (or 14...hxg4 15 h5! gxh5 16 ♕g5+ ♔h8 17 ♘d5 wins) 15 gxh5 ♘xh5 16 ♖dg1 ♖h8 17 ♖g5 c6 18 ♖hg1 ♕f6 19 ♘f5+!

(the threat to the d6 pawn forces Black to exchange pieces) 19...♗xf5 20 exf5 ♖h6 21 ♘e4 ♘xe4 22 fxe4 ♔h7 23 ♗xh5 gxh5 24 ♕g2 1-0.

Also possible is 8...♕e7 to wait and see how White intends to attack. Horn-Umbach, Zürich 1992 continued: 9 ♗xg7 ♔xg7 10 ♗d3 (over-protecting the e4 pawn before carrying out an advance of the kingside pawns) 10...c6 11 h3 ♖e8 12 ♕e3 b6 13 ♘d2 ♗b7 14 f4 ♖ad8 15 dxe5 dxe5 16 f5 ♘c5 17 ♗e2 ♖d7 18 g4 with an impressive pawn storm.

9 ♕xh6 ♘g4

Black wants the eject the enemy queen from the kingside before White has time to play ♘f3-g5 with a firm grip on the position. The only snag is that the weak dark squares around the black king are a long-term concern.

10 ♕d2 exd4 11 ♘xd4 ♕f6?!

The queen attacks f2 but the text move is really designed to add support to Black's beleaguered king. However it takes away an important retreat square for the knight on g4 and so perhaps instead 11...♖e8 should be considered.

12 f4 a6

Though it prevents a white knight coming to b5, 12...c6 is not much of an improvement because 13 h3 ♘h6 14 g4 ♕e7 15 g5 wins.

13 h3 ♕h4

A horrible-looking move, which pins the h-pawn but ultimately just exposes the black queen. It seems there is nothing better as after 13...♘h6 14 g4 (threatening a fork by g4-g5) 14...♕e7 15 g5 and the knight runs out of decent squares.

14 g3 ♕h6

If 14...♕xg3 then 15 hxg4 wins a piece.

15 ♗g2 ♘gf6 16 g4

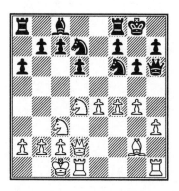

White advances his kingside pawns to provoke weaknesses and launch a big attack. Black is in trouble because of his poor defence which is hardly helped by the fact that his queenside pieces take no active part in the game.

16...♕g7 17 g5 ♘e8 18 h4

Now Spraggett wants to open the h-file for his rooks.

18...♘b6 19 h5 gxh5?!

19...♗d7 at least forces White to reveal his attacking plan, the simplest of which is 20 ♖h2 followed by doubling rooks on the h-file.

20 ♗h3 c5 21 ♘f5 ♗xf5 22 ♗xf5 ♕d4

Black has grabbed a pawn in the knowledge that his real test will come on the h-file which White will soon dominate. The position is hopeless for Black.

23 ♕e2 1-0

The success of the 150 Attack has been so great that even Garry Kasparov has adopted it. One commentator suggested after the following game that the opening should now be known as the 2800 Attack!

Kasparov-Radjabov
FIDE Grand Prix, Moscow 2002

1 d4 ♘f6 2 ♘f3 g6 3 ♘c3 ♗g7 4 e4 d6 5 ♗e3 c6 6 ♕d2

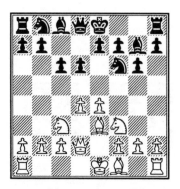

6...♘bd7

As usual I have adopted our accepted move-order to avoid confusion. The original sequence was 1 e4 g6 2 d4 ♗g7 3 ♘c3 c6 4 ♘f3 d6 5 ♗e3 ♘d7 6 ♕d2 ♘gf6.

Other moves are:

a) 6...♕a5 7 h3 ♘bd7 8 a3 0-0 9 ♗d3 e5 10 0-0 with a slight edge, Hebden-McNab, British Team Ch (4NCL) 2002.

b) 6...b5 7 ♗d3 ♘bd7 8 ♗h6 ♗xh6 9 ♕xh6 e5 10 0-0 ♕e7 11 a4 b4 12 ♘e2 a5 13 ♘g3 ♗b7 14 c3 when White is better because Black's king is vulnerable, Zhang Zhong-Simonenko, Ubeda 2001.

c) 6...♗g4 and now:

c1) 7 ♘g1!? (an odd-looking move but the idea is to push away the bishop on g4 and then carry on developing) 7... 0-0 8 h3 ♗c8 9 ♗h6 b5 10 ♗xg7 ♔xg7 11 ♗d3 (White needs to protect the e4 pawn in view of the possibility of ...b5-b4) 11...e5 12 dxe5 dxe5 13 ♘f3 ♘bd7 14 a4 b4 15 ♘e2 c5 16 ♕e3 with roughly equal chances, Carlier-Seret, Montpellier 2001.

c2) 7 ♗e2 (White wants to make sure his kingside pawn structure is not damaged by a black capture on f3) 7...0-0 8 0-0 ♘bd7 9 a4 ♕c7 10 h3 ♗xf3 11 ♗xf3 e5 12 a5 with an edge, Pein-Graham, British Team Ch (4NCL) 2001.

7 ♗h6

This is in keeping with the basic plan of exchanging the dark-squared bishops to strip Black of an important defensive piece.

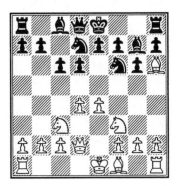

7...♗xh6

Black decides not to test Kasparov's attacking prowess and exchanges bishops rather than castle kingside. A look at the games featuring 7...0-0 sheds light on his thinking:

a) 8 ♗c4 e5 9 0-0-0 ♘g4 (9...b5!? to start some counterplay on the queenside looks sensible) 10 ♗xg7 ♔xg7 11 ♘g5 ♘b6 (11...b5 12 ♗xf7! ♖xf7? 13 ♘e6+ wins) 12 ♗b3 ♔g8?! 13 h4 ♕f6 14 f3 ♘h6 15 h5 ♔h8 (15...exd4 16 ♘e2 c5 17 hxg6 ♕xg6 18 ♖h4 intending to double rooks on the h-file is strong) 16 hxg6 ♕xg6 17 ♖h4 f5 18 ♖dh1 f4 19 ♖xh6 ♕xg5 20 ♖xh7 mate 1-0 Ries-Corde, Paris 1999.

b) 8 ♗xg7 ♚xg7 9 ♗d3 e5 10 0-0 ♕b6 11 ♘a4 ♕c7 12 ♖fe1 ♘b6 13 ♘xb6 (13 ♘c3 ♗g4 is equal) 13...axb6 14 ♕c3 ♖e8 15 h3 with a slight edge, Lutz-Kasimdzhanov, Batumi 2001.

8 ♕xh6

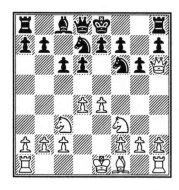

8...e5

A logical idea to challenge the centre which is a principal theme in the Pirc. Also possible:

a) 8...♕a5 9 ♗d3 ♕h5 10 ♕d2 (White wants to attack—not enter an ending!) 10...c5 11 ♗e2 cxd4 (Black has to be careful not to allow the queen to be trapped: 11...0-0 12 ♘g1 ♕h4 13 g3 wins) 12 ♘xd4 ♕c5 13 f4 ♘b6 14 0-0-0 ♗d7 15 ♘b3 (White gains time chasing the black queen, leaving him ahead in development and able to create more tactical opportunities) 15...♕f2 16 e5! dxe5 17 fxe5 ♘h5 18 ♖hf1 ♕xg2 19 ♖xf7! 0-0-0 (or 19...♚xf7 20 ♗c4+ ♘xc4 21 ♕xg2 winning) 20 ♕e3 ♗c6 21 ♘d4 ♘d5 22 ♘xd5 ♕xd5 23 ♗g4+ ♚b8 24 ♘e6 1-0 Arzumanian-Zakharevich, Tula 2002.

b) 8...b5 9 ♗d3 b4 10 ♘e2 ♕c7 11 ♘g3 e5 12 dxe5 dxe5 13 0-0 ♘c5? 14 ♕g7 ♚e7 15 ♕xh8 ♘e6 (Black hopes to play ...♗b7 trapping the white queen) 16 ♘h4 when the threat of either knight checking on f5 allows the queen to escape—with a winning position for White, Yu Shaoteng-Gauthier, D'Agneaux Saint Lo 2001.

9 0-0-0 ♕e7

Radjabov cannot castle kingside so he gradually clears the back rank in order to castle on the other side of the board. If 9...♘g4 then 10 ♕d2 0-0 11 h3 ♘gf6? 12 dxe5 dxe5 13 ♘xe5 reveals one of the tactics available in this line.

10 h3

A calm move ruling out the possibility of ...♞g4.

10...a6?!

It is probably best to play 10...b5 to keep the light-squared bishop away from the c4 square when 11 ♗d3 a6 12 ♖he1 gives White a slight advantage.

11 dxe5 dxe5 12 ♗c4

White activates the bishop and aims at the vulnerable f7 square.

12...b5

The quest for an extra pawn with 12...♛c5?! is a risky venture. For instance 13 ♗b3 ♛xf2? 14 ♖df1 ♛c5 (14...♛xg2? allows 15 ♖hg1 trapping the white queen) 15 ♞g5 ♖f8 16 ♗xf7+! ♖xf7 17 ♞xf7 ♚xf7 18 ♛xh7+ with a terrific attack.

13 ♗b3 a5 14 a4! b4 15 ♞b1 ♗a6

15...♞xe4 has been suggested when 16 ♛e3 has been put forward by commentators but it is not clear how White can try to win. Instead I think the aggressive line starting with 16 ♖he1 gives White the advantage. For example: 16...f5 17 ♞bd2!! (17 ♖xe4?! fxe4 18 ♞g5 just fails to impress after 18...♛f8 when Black is hanging on) 17...♞xf2 (17...♞xd2 18 ♖xd2 threatening ♞xe5 followed by ♖de2 when 18...e4 19 ♞g5 is good for White) 18 ♞c4 ♞e4 (18...♞xd1 runs into 19 ♞cxe5 and Black's position collapses) 19 ♖xe4! fxe4 20 ♞fxe5 ♞xe5 21 ♞d6+ ♚d8 22 ♞f5+ ♛d7 23 ♖xd7+ ♞xd7 24 ♞g7! when White is better because Black's pieces lack harmony.

16 ♞bd2 0-0-0

Black finally finds time to castle but the pawns in front of his king are already too advanced to provide cover for his king.

17 ♛e3! ♚b7

If Black blocks access to a7 with 17...♞c5 then 18 ♗xf7 ♞xa4 (18...♛xf7 19 ♛xc5 is fantastic for White) 19 ♗c4 ♗b7 20 ♞b3 and White is on top.

18 ♗c4

Kasparov wants to install a knight on c4 but an immediate 18 ♞c4 will be met by ♗xc4. Therefore he seeks to exchange bishops before moving the knight to c4.

18...♞c5?

18...♞b6 is necessary to stop White activating his queen's knight.

19 ♗xa6+ ♚xa6

20 ♘c4!

The knight heads towards Black's position and his weakened pawn structure is the target.

20...♘fxe4

If 20...♘xa4 then White can use his knights to great tactical effect after 21 ♘fxe5 ♛c5 22 ♛e2 ♛b5 23 ♘xf7 ♖xd1+ 24 ♖xd1 ♖f8 25 ♘fd6 winning.

21 ♘fxe5 ♖d5

21...b3 is a spirited attempt to create counterplay but it can be refuted by 22 ♘xc6 ♖xd1+ 23 ♖xd1 ♛f6 24 ♘6xa5 bxc2 25 ♔xc2 ♛f5 26 g4 and Black can go home. Or 21...♛e6 22 ♛e2! (22 f3 is not convincing after 22...f6 23 fxe4 ♘xa4) 22...f5 23 ♘f7 ♖xd1+ (23...♛xf7 24 ♘d6+ wins) 24 ♖xd1 ♖e8 25 ♘fe5 ♔a7 26 ♛e3 threatening f3 and ♖d6 winning.

22 ♘xc6

White starts collecting pawns—and against Kasparov that is bad news.

22...♛g5 23 ♖xd5 ♛xd5 24 ♘4xa5 ♔b6 25 ♘xb4 1-0

SUMMARY

The 150 Attack is certainly an awkward system for Black to meet. It is clear that this simple set-up is outstandingly effective and there is no refutation otherwise Kasparov would not have given it his seal of approval. The game **Spraggett-Gonzalez Amaya** is a good example of what happens when Black castles kingside. White is able to exchange dark-squared bishops to weaken the kingside and eventually start a kingside pawn advance. **Kasparov-Radjabov** is a high-class encounter where White follows the basic plan of undermining the defence of the kingside which prompts Black to castle on the other flank. White's speedy development and aggressive style reaps the deserved reward.

ODD OPENINGS

I think that any reader will enjoy playing the London System or Barry Attack where they can enter familiar territory and are able to play their favourite lines. But what happens when Black plays something strange? A quick glance at the following games will give an insight into some of the popular sidelines which are used by club players as surprise weapons. It is worth remembering that Black is usually relying on eccentric, trappy moves, which can be easily foiled if you know the right way to respond.

THE HISTORY OF THE ENGLUND GAMBIT

The standard sequence is 1 d4 e5 2 dxe5 ♘c6 3 ♘f3 ♛e7 and was named after the Swedish player Fritz Englund (1871-1933). It has never really caught on at the top level even though players such as Keres did try it out. However, it has proved to be a very effective weapon at club level with players of the white pieces failing to cope at the board with some of the tricks available to Black. It seems to have had its fair share of popularity in Germany thanks to the tireless efforts of FM Stefan Bücker who has extensively played and written about this relatively little known opening.

IDEAS BEHIND THE OPENING

Perhaps the greatest merit of the opening is that Black is guaranteed a chance to play it on move one. There is something to be said for this because at least White is then obliged to enter the Englund and cope with the various difficulties. The classic trick of the opening has been used to win numerous games and is still catching people out:

Deacon-Katnić
Toukley 2002

1 d4 e5 2 dxe5 ♘c6 3 ♘f3 ♛e7 4 ♗f4

Superficially it seems that White is able to support the e-pawn and remain a pawn up.

4...♛b4+

Making full use of the queen's unorthodox position on e7. Now Black can get his pawn back.

5 ♗d2?

White could play 5 ♘bd2 to speed up development but White has missed something

5...♕xb2 6 ♗c3 ♗b4!

Black is already winning after just six moves!

7 ♕d2 ♗xc3 8 ♘xc3

At this moment in the game I noticed White looking rather embarrassed because the intended 8 ♕xc3 is hammered by 8...♕c1 mate.

8...♕xa1+ 0-1

HOW TO BEAT THE ENGLUND GAMBIT

The secret of dealing with such an offbeat opening is to treat it with respect. The games where Black emerges with credit tend to be those where White tries to hang on to the extra e-pawn. A better idea is to try and exploit the position of the queen on e7 by developing quickly and castling kingside. Though this sounds too simplistic it makes sense when one considers that Black's queen gets in the way of her own pieces.

Palliser-Sedgwick

Isle of Man 2000

1 d4 e5 2 dxe5 ♘c6 3 ♘f3

White develops a piece and defends the extra pawn. Instead 3 f4 has a relatively poor record because it is Black who gains a lead in development after 3...f6! 4 exf6 ♘xf6 5 ♘c3 d5 6 e3 ♗b4 intending to castle kingside with reasonable chances.

3...♕e7

This is the starting point of the Englund Gambit.

4 ♘c3

White sensibly rejects hanging on to the extra pawn and instead carries on developing. A wise idea bearing in mind that awkward position of the black queen...

4...♘xe5 5 e4 c6

A natural reaction to the unwelcome prospect of ♘c3-d5 although 5...♘f6!? might be considered when 6 ♗e2 is reasonable for White. 5...♘xf3+ was tested in Barredo-Gonzalez Tasis, Santa Olaya 1998, but after 6 ♕xf3 White has good chances. For instance: 6...c6 (6...b6? has been tried a few times but I think that 7 ♘d5! will put it out of business because White is winning after 7...♕c5 {7...♕d8 8 ♕c3 c6 9 ♕e5+ followed by ♘c7+ and Black can give up} 8 ♗e3 ♕a5+ 9 ♗d2 ♕c5 10 b4 ♕c6 11 ♗b5 ♕b7 12 ♗f4 ♗d6 13 ♗xd6 cxd6 14 ♕g3 when the twin threats against d6 and g7 give White a winning position) 7 ♗f4 g6 (if 7...d5 then 8 0-0-0 is fine for White) 8 0-0-0 ♗g7 9 ♗c4 b5 10 ♘xb5! cxb5 11 ♗d5 (the rook has nowhere to hide) 11...♕b4 12 ♕b3 and White wins.

6 ♘xe5

Palliser draws the black queen out into the open. I also like the simple 6 ♗e2 intending kingside castling followed by ♘f3-d4 and f2-f4 to highlight Black's clumsy attempts at development.

6...♕xe5 7 f4 ♕c7?!

The black queen needs to remain active so 7...♕a5 should be considered although 8 ♗c4 ♗b4 9 ♗d2 is still better for White who has the superior development.

8 ♗e3 ♗b4 9 ♕d4! ♗xc3+

Sedgwick has little choice but to give up the bishop and submit to future dark square problems. Of course 9...♗f8 would be the ultimate humiliation.

10 ♕xc3 ♘f6 11 ♗d3

White defends the e-pawn by bringing another piece into action. White's advantage in space and time is the main theme of the opening. Thus White can mobilise his forces quickly whereas Black struggles to catch up in development.

11...0-0 12 0-0 ♖e8 13 ♗d4

A crafty move—White targets the knight and tempts Black into grabbing a pawn.

13...♘xe4 14 ♖ae1!

An excellent move that pins the knight and hastens Black's demise. Of course, the queen is now taboo because of 14...♘xc3 15 ♖xe8 mate. This tactic has been made possible due to Black's problems with development —in particular the queenside.

14...f5 15 ♗xe4 fxe4 16 ♗xg7

Material may be numerically equal but by capturing the g-pawn White dominates the a1-h8 diagonal and places Black's exposed king in mortal danger.

16...d5 17 ♗e5 ♕f7 18 ♖e3

The rook enters the action and prepares to swing across to g3 to attack the black king.

18...♛f5 19 ♖g3+

Palliser now has all the fun and goes on a king-hunt.

19...♚f7 20 ♖g5

A winning move but a more clinical finish would have been 20 ♖g7+ ♚e6 21 g4 and Black can give up.

20...♛e6 21 ♖g7+ ♚f8 22 ♛a3+ ♖e7 23 ♖xe7 ♛xe7 24 ♗d6 1-0

THE HISTORY OF THE CLARENDON COURT

This opening that occurs after **1 d4 c5 2 d5 f5!?** has been known for some time but recently experienced an upsurge of popularity after a number of British players used it successfully in tournaments around the world. Their motivation sprung from the fertile brain of grandmaster Jonathan Levitt who regularly adopted the variation and even wrote articles to bring it to the attention of a wider audience. Nevertheless modesty prevented him from calling it the 'Levitt opening' and instead he named it after the apartment block in London where he lives! Surely the only chess opening that also serves as a private address.

IDEAS BEHIND THE OPENING

Levitt adopted the idea as a way of playing a kind of accelerated Dutch, the rationale being that the move-order reduces the effectiveness of the annoying continuations 2 ♗g5 and 2 ♘c3. The Clarendon Court also produces a set-up similar to the Leningrad Dutch but where Black has the bonus of a long range fianchettoed bishop thanks to the advance of the white d-pawn.

HOW TO BEAT THE CLARENDON COURT

I recommend 3 e4 as to way to put instant pressure on the Clarendon Court set-up.

I had a look at other continuations such as 3 ♘c3 and 3 g3, which are reasonable but allow Black to have his own way. But when I examined a line that can pose immediate problems for Black in a normal Dutch—1 d4 f5 2 e4—I noticed a critical difference when this was applied to the Clarendon Court...

Schlosser-Bischoff
Austrian Team Championship 1997

1 d4 c5 2 d5 f5

3 e4!

The role model for this move comes from the Staunton Gambit in the Dutch. This can occur after 1 d4 f5 2 e4 when a sample line is 2...fxe4 3 ♘c3 ♘f6 4 g4 h6 5 ♗g2 after which Black supports the e-pawn with ...d7-d5. The difference in the line I recommend is that with a white pawn already on d5 it is not so easy to protect a black pawn landing on e4.

I also tried to borrow the idea 1 d4 f5 2 g4 and incorporate it into a fighting line against the Clarendon Court. However, though I do not think it is as strong as the text, it can create problems for Black due to White's space advantage and open lines. For instance: 3 g4 fxg4 4 e4 d6 5 h3 ♘f6 (5...gxh3 6 ♗xh3 ♗xh3 7 ♘xh3 ♘f6 8 ♘g5, heading for e6, is awkward for Black) 6 ♘c3 g6 (6...♕a5!?, making use of the early ...c7-c5, looks useful) 7 hxg4 ♗xg4 8 f3 ♗c8 (8...♗d7!? is a possible alternative) 9 ♘h3 ♗g7 10 ♘f4 ♘a6 11 ♗b5+ ♔f7 (Black is obliged to forfeit the right to castle because 11...♗d7 is crushed by 12 ♘e6) 12 a4 ♘c7 13 ♗c4 ♖e8 14 ♕e2 e5 15 dxe6+ ♗xe6 16 ♘xe6 ♘xe6 17 ♗g5 with sufficient compensation for the pawn due to the fragile state of the black king, B.Jones-Valenti, Canberra 2001. However, as indicated, Black has scope for improvement.

3...fxe4 4 ♘c3 ♘f6

4...g6 shows that Black is willing to hand back the pawn provided that this enables him to develop his kingside. He is hoping for 5 ♘xe4 d6 6 ♘f3 ♗g7 with roughly equal chances. However, 5 h4! is the strongest response, which casts doubt on Black's move-order. Rashkovsky-Musalov, Biel 2001, continued 5...♗g7 6 h5 (White already has the initiative and is ready to weaken black's kingside pawn structure) 6...♕b6 (6...gxh5? 7 ♕xh5+ ♔f8 8 ♘xe4 ♘f6 9 ♘xf6 exf6 10 ♗f4 gives White the advantage) 7 ♘ge2 d6 8 ♘xe4 ♘a6 (8...♗xb2 9 ♖b1 ♕a5+ 10 ♗d2 ♕xa2 11 ♖xb2! ♕xb2 12 ♗c3 and Black is busted) 9 c3 ♗d7 10 ♘f4 0-0-0 11 ♘g5! (White is determined to place a knight on the important e6 square where it can dominate the board) 11...♖f8 12 ♘fe6 ♗xe6 13 ♘xe6 ♖f7 14 hxg6 hxg6 15 ♖xh8 ♗xh8 16 ♕g4 c4 17 ♘d4+ ♔b8 18 ♕xg6 gave White a winning advantage.

5 g4

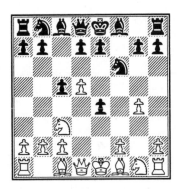

White advances the g-pawn and intends g5 to chase away the knight which is defending e4.

5 ♗g5 is occasionally seen but has not really caught on at tournament level: 5...d6 6 ♗xf6?! (White should gambit the pawn with 6 ♕d2!? intending 0-0-0 and f2-f3) 6...exf6 7 ♘xe4 ♗e7 8 ♗d3 f5 9 ♘c3 0-0 10 ♘f3 ♘d7 11 0-0 ♘e5 is fine for Black.

5...h6

Black wants to deter White from advancing the g-pawn and ousting his knight. Also possible:

a) 5...g6 is popular due to the well known game Matros-Ehlvest, Stockholm 1999, where Black returned the pawn and used his active pieces to triumph. It is worth looking at a model example of what White should avoid: 6 g5 ♘h5 7 ♘xe4?! d6 8 ♘g3 ♘xg3 9 hxg3 (the semi-open h-file for the king's rook gives White decent tactical chances but he still needs to get his pieces into the action) 9...♘d7 10 ♘h3 ♕b6 11 f4?! (11 c3, intending to use the f4 square for the knight, is an improvement) 11...♕b4+! 12 ♔f2 (12 ♕d2/♗d2 ♕e4+ and Black wins a whole rook) 12...♕d4+ 13 ♗e3?! (White is keen on the idea of attack but circumstances dictate he should enter the ending by 13 ♕xd4 cxd4 14 ♗d2 ♗g7 with roughly equal chances) 13...♕xb2 14 a4 ♗g7 15 ♖b1 ♕a2 16 ♘g1 (a quick glance at White's badly placed pieces is reason enough to rightly assume that Black stands clearly better) 16...♘b6 17 ♗d3 ♔d8 18 ♘e2 ♕xd5 and with two extra pawns Black won quickly. However I believe White can profit from Black blindly trying to follow this example because the improvement 7 ♗e2! forces the knight to retreat. Then play might continue 7...♘g7 8 h4 ♘f5 9 h5 with an edge.

b) 5...d6 is met by 6 g5, e.g.

b1) 6...♘g4? 7 ♗b5+! ♔f7 (7...♗d7? allows 8 ♕xg4 winning a piece) 8 ♘xe4 with advantage to White because Black cannot castle.

b2) 6...♘fd7 7 ♘xe4 ♘b6 8 ♗f4 e5? 9 dxe6 d5 (the d-pawn escapes capture but Black walks into a nasty trap) 10 ♘f6+! ♔e7 (if 10...gxf6 then 11 ♕h5+ ♔e7 12 ♕f7 mate) 11 ♕h5 ♗xe6 12 ♘xh7 ♘c6 13 0-0-0 ♔d7 14 ♗h3 ♕e8 15 ♘f6+ is clearly winning, Rajković-Martinović, Yugoslav Team Ch 1995.

6 ♗g2 e6!?

The alternative 6...♕b6 sets an amusing trap: 7 ♘ge2! (not falling for 7 ♘xe4?? ♘xe4 8 ♗xe4 ♕b4+ and White can pack away the pieces) 7...d6 (7...♘xg4 8 ♘f4! highlights the weakness of the g6 square: 8...♘f6 9 ♘g6 ♖g8 10 0-0 with decent compensation for the pawn) 8 h3 g5 9 ♘xe4 ♘xe4 10 ♗xe4 ♕b4+ 11 ♘c3 ♗g7 12 ♗d2 ♕xb2 (12...♗xc3?? 13 ♗g6+ ♔d8 14 ♗xc3 wins or 12...0-0?! 13 ♕e2 ♕xb2 14 ♖b1 ♕a3 15 ♖b3 ♕a5 16 h4 with a killer attack) 13 ♖b1 ♕a3 14 ♖b3 ♕a6 (if 14...♕a5 then 15 ♕e2 maintains the initiative) 15 ♘b5 ♔d8 (15...♕b6?! 16 ♘d4 ♕c7 17 ♗g6+ ♔d8 18 ♘b5 gives White active piece play) 16 ♕e2 b6 17 0-0 ♘d7 18 a4! when the combination of the isolated black queen and stranded king gives White more than enough compensation for the pawn, Conquest-Becerra Rivero, Havana 1996.

Or 6...d6 7 ♘xe4! ♘xg4 8 h3 ♘f6 (8...♘e5 9 f4 ♘f7 10 ♕h5 ♕d7 11 ♘g3! e5 12 ♘1e2 maintains the tension) 9 ♘xf6+ exf6 (after 9...gxf6 10 ♕h5+ ♔d7 11 ♘e2 White is still better) 10 ♕h5+ ♔d7 11 ♘e2 when Black will have difficulties developing with the king on such a silly square.

7 ♘ge2 d6 8 h3 ♘bd7?!

An oversight because White's positional trick is not obvious. If 8...♗e7 then 9 ♘f4 ensures the knight is well placed to take advantage of the vacant g6 square. 8...♕a5 pinning the knight is a possible improvement although after 9 0-0 I prefer White's chances due to his superior development and potential attacking chances.

9 dxe6!

9 ♘f4, heading for the g6 square, is not so good in this position: 9...exd5 10 ♘g6 ♖g8 11 ♘xd5 ♘xd5 12 ♕xd5 ♘f6 13 ♕d1 d5 and Black retains the extra pawn with the advantage.

9...♘e5 10 ♘xe4 ♗xe6

10...♘xe4 is not much help after 11 ♗xe4 ♗xe6 12 ♗xb7 and it is White who is a clear pawn up.

11 ♘f4 ♗f7

11...♗c8 looks ugly but at least saves the pawn on b7 although 12 ♘xf6+ ♕xf6 13 ♘d5 plants a strong knight on d5 when 13...♕d8 14 f4 ♘c6 15 ♕d3 is very good.

12 ♘xf6+ ♕xf6 13 ♗xb7

The opening against the German grandmaster has been a complete success. White is a pawn up with the advantage.

13...♖b8 14 ♗g2 g5 15 ♘d5 ♕d8 16 0-0 ♗g7 17 ♘e3

A great move because it plunges Black into a dilemma as to how to cope with the threat of ♘f5.

17...♘g6

Bischoff is ready to meet 18 ♘f5 with 18...♗e5 but now he has to give up the right to castle.

18 ♗c6+ ♔f8 19 ♗d5 ♗xd5 20 ♘xd5 ♗xb2 21 ♗xb2 ♖xb2

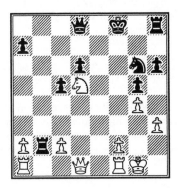

Black might have restored the material balance but the perilous position of his king is the decisive factor.

22 f4! ♘xf4 23 ♘xf4 gxf4 24 ♖xf4+ ♔g7 25 ♕f3 ♕e7 26 ♖d1 ♖b7 27 ♖e4 ♕g5 28 h4

The final piece of the jigsaw is completed and the queen is overloaded with defensive duties.

28...♕g6 29 h5 1-0

Black cannot put up much resistance with 29...♕g5 because 30 ♖e6 is clearly winning.

THE ST GEORGE

HISTORY OF THE ST. GEORGE

The St. George can occur when 1 d4 is met by the outrageous 1...b5, which has been played numerous times as a surprise weapon by club players and even former world title contender Nigel Short. After 2 e4, to take over the centre, Black calmly replies 2...a6. It looks silly but it has a decent pedigree and can also occur after 1 d4 and then 1...a6—so you have been warned. The naming of openings is a controversial issue but few would argue about the St. George. The maverick English chess master Michael Basman christened it after seeing the infamous game where world champion Karpov was humiliated by Tony Miles who met 1 e4 with the astonishing 1...a6. The name was a reminder of the fact that this opening had been developed by English players and had subsequently been used in a heroic encounter. How could anyone play such a silly opening against Karpov who at the time reigned supreme and was renowned for his well thought out opening repertoire? Basman later revealed that Miles had been experimenting with Owen's Defence—1 e4 b6 with a queenside fianchetto —and had had a few encouraging results. This prompted Miles to analyse Basman's pet line and start to develop new ideas. The St. George refers to the patron saint of England and Tony Miles' birthday was on the 23rd April, which is also St. George's Day.

IDEAS BEHIND THE OPENING

In our context the St. George usually arises after 1 d4 b5 2 e4 ♗b7 when, despite his rather eccentric opening choice, Black can obtain reasonable practical chances by challenging the white centre. Here is the game that made the national television news in England and sent a chuckle through the chess world...

Karpov-Miles
European Team Championship, Skara 1980

1 e4 a6

After playing this shock move Miles noticed that not only had the large audience broke out into a collective mutter but also that his opponent's ears had turned bright red. However, though Karpov later admitted that he had felt personally insulted by 1...a6, it was a choice that Miles had carefully made some time before as a means of upsetting his opponent's excellent opening preparation. And if it is good enough to beat Karpov you can bet it will do the business at the local chess club...

2 d4 b5

In his comments to the game Tony wrote "By this time the spectators' laughing was becoming embarrassing".

3 ♘f3 ♗b7

The inspiration of Owen's Defence! The bishop again targets the e4 pawn but now Black can also claim space on the queenside.

4 ♗d3 ♘f6 5 ♕e2 e6 6 a4!?

Trying to refute the opening by quickly undermining the advanced b-pawn.

6...c5 7 dxc5

7 e5 is met by 7...c4 to exchange the light-squared bishop—traditionally a key attacking piece in this sort of position.

7...♗xc5 8 ♘bd2 b4 9 e5 ♘d5 10 ♘e4 ♗e7 11 0-0?!

A critical move is 11 ♗g5! threatening ♘d6+ as the bishop on e7 will be pinned. For example: 11...0-0 (11...f6?! 12 exf6 gxf6 13 ♘e5! intending ♕h5 with advantage) 12 ♘d6 ♗c6 intending ...f7-f6 with slightly better prospects for White.

11...♘c6 12 ♗d2

Now 12 ♗g5 is less impressive because Black has developed an extra piece—which makes a difference after 12...f6 13 exf6 gxf6 14 ♗h6 (14 ♘e5, making way for ♕h5 as given in the previous note, is now useless because of 14...♘xe5) 14...♕c7 with roughly equal chances.

12...♕c7 13 c4 bxc3 14 ♘xc3 ♘xc3 15 ♗xc3 ♘b4!

Black is keen to deprive White of the bishop pair.

16 ♗xb4 ♗xb4 17 ♖ac1 ♕b6 18 ♗e4 0-0

The position can be assessed as equal. However Karpov was still fuming over the 'insult' and, without real justification, decided to go on the attack.

19 ♘g5

The Greek Gift idea of 19 ♗xh7+ is tempting but fails to impress after 19...♔xh7 20 ♘g5+ ♔g6! 21 ♕g4 f5 22 ♕g3 ♕d4 23 h3 (to stop the queen blocking the check on g4) 23...♔h5 and the black king should escape, leaving White a piece down.

19...h6 20 ♗h7+ ♔h8 21 ♗b1 ♗e7 22 ♘e4 ♖ac8 23 ♕d3?

Lining up for a checkmate on h7 but Miles has seen further.

23...♖xc1 24 ♖xc1 ♕xb2 25 ♖e1 ♕xe5 26 ♕xd7

White is a clear pawn down and must have been thinking of just one move as his position went rapidly downhill. The move? Why, 1...a6 of course!

26...♗b4 27 ♖e3 ♕d5

Miles forces White to exchange queens and enter a lost ending. At the time Tony was one of the top players in the world and the result is never in doubt. The game concluded:

28 ♕xd5 ♗xd5 29 ♘c3 ♖c8 30 ♘e2 g5 31 h4 ♔g7 32 hxg5 hxg5 33 ♗d3 a5 34 ♖g3 ♔f6 35 ♖g4 ♗d6 36 ♔f1 ♗e5 37 ♔e1 ♖h8 38 f4 gxf4 39 ♘xf4 ♗c6 40 ♘e2 ♖h1+ 41 ♔d2 ♖h2 42 g3 ♗f3 43 ♖g8 ♖g2 44 ♔e1 ♗xe2 45 ♗xe2 ♖xg3 46 ♖a8 ♗c7 0-1

HOW TO BEAT THE ST. GEORGE

I think the best policy is to keep faith with the London System. The pawn on b5 is rather a liability if Black cannot use his queenside fianchetto to target the pawn on e4. As usual White will rapidly develop via the familiar pawn structure. Even if it is best to play 2 e4, that would entail learning a chunk of theory on an opening which will only occur occasionally.

Heinl-Wolf
Baden 1997

1 d4 b5 2 ♘f3 ♗b7 3 ♗f4

"If in doubt—play the London System!" should be your motto.

3...e6

Black prepares to develop the king's bishop. Also possible:

a) 3...a6 4 ♘bd2 e6 5 e4 (White cannot resist the temptation to take over the centre but 5 e3 is also fine) 5...d6 6 ♗d3 ♘d7 7 ♕e2 ♗e7 8 h3 c5 9 c3 when White had a space advantage, Gamble-G.Lee, Southend 1998.

b) 3...♘f6 4 h3 e6 5 e3 c5 6 ♘bd2 a6 7 a4 (having developed his pieces in the standard way, White aims to undermine the black queenside pawns) 7...bxa4 8 ♖xa4 ♘c6 9 ♗e2 ♗e7 10 0-0 ♘d5 11 ♗h2 with a small plus, Plumanns-Sulskis, Budapest 1996.

4 e3

White attacks the b-pawn and Black must do something about it.

4...a6

4...b4 is an obvious way to evade capture but it also makes the pawn more vulnerable. For example: 5 ♘bd2 ♘f6 6 ♗d3 ♗e7 7 h3 0-0 8 0-0 (as usual White employs the traditional set-up to get his pieces into play) 8...d6 9 e4 ♘bd7 10 ♕e2 ♖e8 11 e5 ♘d5 12 ♗h2 gave White the better chances due to the threats against h7, Holscher-Mook, Haarlem 2001. I was shocked to see 4...c6?! in Mourgues-Carlier, St Affrique 1999—a bizarre way to defend the b-pawn and with the plan of developing his pieces behind a wall of pawns. That game went 5 ♗d3 ♘f6 6 h3 ♗e7 7 0-0 0-0 8 ♘bd2 (the opening strategy has been easy for White who has simply followed the usual plan of action in the London System) 8...d6 9 c3 ♘bd7 10 a4 with an edge.

5 ♗d3

It makes sense to keep developing the pieces although 5 a4 is also perfectly acceptable. For instance: 5...b4 6 ♘bd2 ♘f6 7 ♗d3 (this system of development is an echo of the main game) 7...c5 8 c3 (8 0-0!? is a decent alternative) 8...♘c6 9 0-0 ♗e7 10 ♘c4 d5 11 ♘ce5 c4 12 ♘xc6 (12 ♗c2?! b3 13 ♗b1 locks the queen's rook out of the game) 12...♗xc6 13 ♘e5 ♗b7 14 ♗e2 with equal chances, Povah-Tiller, British Team Ch (4NCL) 1999.

5...♘f6

Black can also try 5...f5!? to help secure control over the e4 square. Caessens-Etmans, Dieren 1989, continued 6 0-0 ♘f6 7 ♘bd2 ♗e7 8 c4 (a useful advance of the c-pawn to weaken the black queenside pawns) 8...bxc4 9 ♗xc4 0-0 10 ♖c1 ♗d5? 11 ♗xc7 gave White a clear advantage.

6 0-0 c5 7 dxc5

With a pawn on b5 White is concerned about the prospect of ...c5-c4 closing the position—so he cannot exploit his lead in development.

7...♗xc5 8 ♘bd2 d5 9 ♘e5

The king's knight takes up its traditional outpost on e5.

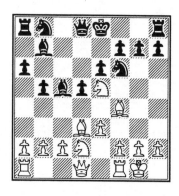

9...♘bd7 10 ♘b3 ♗b6 11 ♘d4!?

White is already better and could try to tackle the queenside pawns by 11 a4 when 11...b4 (11...bxa4 12 ♖xa4 gives White strong pressure against the weak a-pawn) 12 a5 (White gains time and more importantly isolates the b-pawn) 12...♗c7 13 ♘xd7 ♕xd7 14 ♗xc7 ♕xc7 15 ♕d2, intending a quick ♖a4 to attack the weak b-pawn, is better for White.

11...♘c5 12 c3!?

12 ♕f3 to aid a kingside attack looks good.

12...♘xd3 13 ♘xd3 ♘e4 14 ♕g4 ♗xd4?!

An error of judgement because Black need not give up his useful bishop, which merely allows White to dominate the dark squares. Also 14...♕f6, to protect the g7 pawn, leaves Black sliding downhill after 15 ♗e5 h5 16 ♕e2 ♕h6 17 f3 ♘f6 18 ♗f4 ♕h7 19 a4 and White can step up his operations on the queenside while the black queen is far away. Probably best in the circumstances is 14...0-0!? since it is difficult for White to deliver a quick knockout even if Black has 'castled into it'.

15 exd4 g5?!

Black tries to make a fight of it by going for complications but the advance of the kingside pawns represents a long-term weakness.

If 15...0-0 then 16 ♗e5 ♘f6 17 ♕g3, intending ♘c5, gives White a firm hold on the position.

16 ♗e5 h5 17 ♕e2 f6

Wolf is in an awkward position and the obvious 17...♖h7 fails to impress after 18 f3 ♘f6 19 ♘c5 ♗c6 20 a4 when White has the superior chances.

18 f3 fxe5

There is little choice since 18...♘d6 19 ♗g3 ♕e7 20 ♘c5 ♗c8 21 a4 also looks bleak for Black.

19 fxe4 exd4 20 ♕f2!

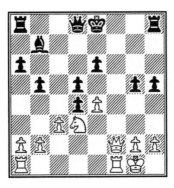

A simple solution for White. The queen not only threatens mate but can also recapture on d4 and dominate the board.

20...♕e7 21 ♕xd4 0-0-0

At long last Wolf tries to shield the king and co-ordinate the rooks but it is too late.

22 e5 ♔b8 23 ♖f6 ♖df8 24 ♖af1 ♖xf6

Naturally Black is reluctant to present White with a strong passed pawn but there is not much else. Black's plight is highlighted after 24...h4 when the strong reply 25 ♕b6 threatens ♘c5, ♘c4 or even taking on e6—all of which are decisive.

25 exf6 ♕d6 26 f7 ♖f8 27 ♘e5 ♔c8 28 ♕b4 1-0

SUMMARY

The Englund Gambit is particularly popular amongst juniors who want to play something tricky after just one move. Therefore the example set by White in the game **Palliser-Sedgwick** is a good model. The key is sensible development, without trying to hold on to the extra pawn, and exploitation of the poorly placed queen on e7. The Clarendon Court has the neat idea of getting an improved version of the Dutch Defence on the board but **Schlosser-Bischoff** demonstrates an adventurous way to cross Black's plans —the gambit 3 e4. The St. George has a remarkable history which includes a victory against a reigning world champion but White can still respond with the trusty plan of development of the London System which has the merit of not providing Black with a target pawn on e4. The game **Heinl-Wolf** explores some of the promising continuations available for White.

INDEX OF VARIATIONS

The Queen's Indian Formations

1 d4 ♘f6 2 ♘f3 e6 3 ♗f4 b6 3...c5 *109* 4 e3 c5 5 ♗d3 ♗b7 6 c3 *105*

The Grünfeld Formations

1 d4 ♘f6 2 ♘f3 g6 3 ♗f4 ♗g7 4 e3 d5 5 ♗d3 c5 5...♗g4/0-0 *118* 6 c3 *118*
                                4 ♘bd2 d5 5 e3 0-0 6 ♗d3 b6 *120*

The King's Indian Defence

1 d4 ♘f6 2 ♘f3 g6 3 ♗f4 ♗g7 4 e3 d6 5 h3 0-0 6 ♗e2 ♘bd7 7 0-0 b6 8 ♗h2 *125*
                                7...e5/♖e8/♘e4 *125* 7...c5 *127*
                                     7...♕e8 8 c4 *130* 8 ♗h2 e5 9 c4 ♘e4 *133*

The Barry Attack

1 d4 ♘f6 2 ♘f3 g6 3 ♘c3 d5 4 ♗f4 ♗g7 5 e3 0-0 5...♘bd7 *138* 6 ♗e2
6...b6 7 ♘e5 ♗b7 8 h4 h6 8...♘bd7*139* 9 h5 *139*
6...c5 7 ♘e5 7 dxc5 *141* 7...cxd4 7...♗e6/♘c6 *141-142* 8 exd4 ♘fd7 8...♘c6 *144*
9 ♘f3 *142*
6...c6 7 h3 ♘bd7 8 0-0 ♖e8 9 ♗h2 *145*
6...♗g4 7 ♘e5 ♗xe2 8 ♕xe2 c6 8...c5 *147* 9 h4 *147*

The 150 Attack

1 d4 ♘f6 2 ♘f3 g6 3 ♘c3 ♗g7 4 e4 d6 5 ♗e3 0-0 6 ♕d2 ♘bd7
6...e5/6...♘g4/a6/♗g4 *151* 7 ♗h6 *152*
5...c6 6 ♕d2 ♘bd7 6...♕a5/b5/♗g4 *155* 7 ♗h6 ♗xh6 7...0-0 *155* 8 ♕xh6 *156*

Odd Openings

1 d4 e5 2 dxe5 ♘c6 3 ♘f3 ♕e7 4 ♘c3 4 ♗f4 *159* 4...♘xe5 5 e4 *161*
1 d4 c5 2 d5 f5 3 e4 fxe4 4 ♘c3 ♘f6 4...g6 *165* 5 g4 h6 5...g6/d6 *165-166*
6 ♗g2 *166*
1 d4 b5 2 ♘f3 ♗b7 3 ♗f4 e6 3...a6/♘f6 4 e3 *171*